ANDREW MEADE

OF IRELAND AND VIRGINIA

Toujours Prêt

Meade

Andrew Meade

of Ireland and Virginia

HIS ANCESTORS, AND SOME OF HIS DESCENDANTS AND THEIR CONNECTIONS

INCLUDING

SKETCHES OF THE FOLLOWING FAMILIES:
MEADE, EVERARD, HARDAWAY,
SEGAR, PETTUS, AND
OVERTON

"We may build more splendid habitations, fill our rooms with paintings and with sculpture, but we cannot buy with gold the old associations." —Longfellow.

by
P. Hamilton Baskervill, A.M. (U. of Va.)
Chiefly from letters, papers, and other material
furnished by Mrs. Elise Meade (Skelton)
Baskervill, and from other sources.

HERITAGE BOOKS
2012

HERITAGE BOOKS

AN IMPRINT OF HERITAGE BOOKS, INC.

Books, CDs, and more—Worldwide

For our listing of thousands of titles see our website
at
www.HeritageBooks.com

A Facsimile Reprint
Published 2012 by
HERITAGE BOOKS, INC.
Publishing Division
100 Railroad Ave. #104
Westminster, Maryland 21157

Originally published:
Richmond, Virginia
Old Dominion Press, Inc., Printers
1921

International Standard Book Numbers
Paperbound: 978-0-7884-1025-3
Clothbound: 978-0-7884-9216-7

Dedicated to my Wife,

Mrs. Elise Meade (Skelton) Baskervill,

through whose interest, information and assistance
this book has been made possible.

TABLE OF CONTENTS

ILLUSTRATIONS

AUTHORITIES

Historiae Ecclesiae, Orderic Vitalis, 1142;
Brittania, Wm. Camden, 1586;
Smith's *History of Cork*, 1750;
Macaulay's *History of England;*
Pepys Diary, 1660;
Dictionary of National Biography;
Lower's *Family Dictionary;*
Armorial Families, Fox-Davis;
Debrett's *Peerage, Baronetage, and Companionage;*
Burke's *Extinct and Dormant Baronetcies;*
Burke's *Peerage;*
Burke's *Landed Gentry;*
Wright's *History of Essex* (England);
Morant's *History of County Essex*, 1768;
Coller's *The People's History of Essex;*
Tuckett's *Devonshire Pedigrees;*
The Plantagenet Roll of the Blood Royal, Marquis of Ruvigny;
Bishop Meade's *Old Churches and Families of Virginia;*
The Chaumiére Papers, David[3] Meade;
Campbell's *History of Virginia;*
Memoirs of Bishop Meade, Bishop Johns;
Bland Papers;
North Carolina Colonial Records;
North Carolina, Chas. L. Rapier;
Brown's *Genesis of America;*
Thomas Hardaway and His Descendants, Mrs. S. D. Hubert, 1906;
Hotten's *Original List of Persons of Quality, &c.*
Howe's *Historical Collections of Virginia;*
Parish Register of Christ Church, Middlesex;
Tyler's *Cradle of the Republic;*

Goode's *Virginia Cousins;*
Some of the Meads, G. C. Callahan;
Southern History Association's pamphlet *Sir Richard Everard, Bt., Gov. of N. Carolina;*
Vestry Book of Upper Parish of Suffolk, Va.;
Bristol Parish Register and Vestry Book;
Library of Universal Knowledge;
More Colonial Homesteads, Marion Harland;
The Travels of John Francis, Marquis de Chastellux in North America;
Virginia County Records;
William and Mary Quarterly;
Virginia Historical Magazine;
Journal of the Virginia House of Burgesses;
Meade Family Tree;
Newspaper Clippings;
Sundry private letters and statements.

PREFACE

The history of every family, who have antecedents, should be written, and this volume has been prepared to preserve and perpetuate some scattered records, which we have collected.

We have the warrant of Scriptures for valuing our descent from distinguished or worthy ancestors. In the first words of the Gospels we find an account of the human lineage of our Lord Jesus Christ. And then in a later gospel it is traced back to the first man, Adam. So that no one need sneer or laugh at reasonable pride of ancestry, as is the tendency with some people. When this occurs, we can pass it by as unworthy of notice. We may think with Longfellow: "We may build more splendid habitations, fill our rooms with paintings and with sculpture, but we can not buy with gold the old associations."

The family sketches contained in this volume were prepared as a part of our history of the Skeltons of Paxton, Va. But because the interests of the Skelton and the Meade families are not identical, and some of the Skeltons are not especially interested in the Meades, and many of the Meades are not particularly interested in the Skeltons, it seems best to make two books of our history, one of the Skeltons and their connections, and the other of the Meades and their connections.

No attempt has been made to make our Meade sketch exhaustive, but the writer, not being a member of this family, which is very large and very much scattered, has confined himself to the earlier history, abroad and in Virginia, and then to those branches, with which his family is connected. He wishes to disclaim any intention to write an exhaustive general history of the family, because he has not the information and facilities, which this would require.

The descendants of SUSANNA EVERARD, the wife of DAVID[2] MEADE, all of them of course, through her participate in the interesting descent from KING EDWARD III of England, (1328-1377), through his son, LIONEL, DUKE OF CLARENCE, and their names should be included in *The Plantagenet Roll of the Blood Royal, The Clarence Volume,* by the Marquis of Ruvigny and Raneval, London, T. C. and E. C. Jack, 1905. But as a matter of fact many of them are omitted there. However, any member of the Meade family, who can trace his lineage back one or two generations, should be able to find his line of connection in our tables.

The Everard history is very interesting on account of its antiquity and remarkable connections. We have followed some of the lines, and many others might be traced. There are no other known descendants of the Everard family in this country.

The other sketches are not much more than outlines, but they will doubtless help any one to make farther investigations. They are intended merely to give general statements of these families, and particularly their connections with the Meades.

It is probably true that no other kind of composition is so liable to error as genealogical history, and some one has said that its chief use, or rather fate is to be corrected. We are aware that some of our statements, as to the Irish history of the Meades, do not accord with statements accepted by some members of the family and published in certain newspaper articles. But we have adopted them, because they seem to be sustained by reliable historical evidence. However, we shall at all times be pleased to have our attention called to all errors, which may be found in this book, historical, typographical, or otherwise, so that they may be corrected, and we may thereby arrive at the truth.

A number of blank pages have been added in the back of the book, where persons may record their own lines when they are not included, or add any additional history, as they may wish.

Some of the lineage tables seem to be incorrectly printed upside down, but a more careful examination will show that they are correctly arranged.   Holding the book sideways with the back from you the tables read properly.

In two retrospective tables for the sake of brevity and conciseness the writer has traced back the descent, beginning with his son as a representative of the latest generation.   It will be an easy task for any descendant to be substituted in his place.

                                        P. H. BASKERVILL.

Richmond, Va., June 20, 1921.

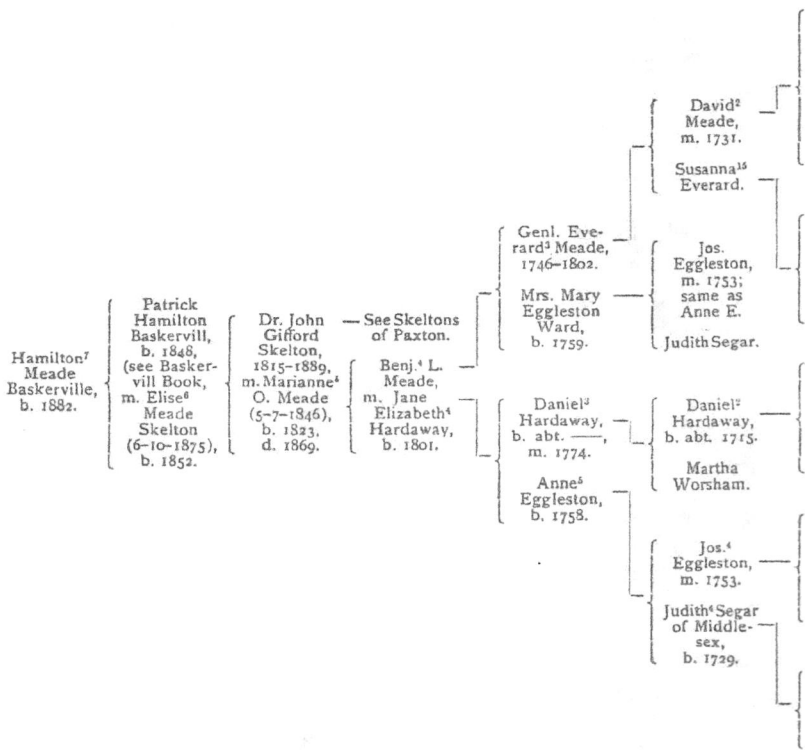

Hamilton⁷
Meade
Baskerville,
b. 1882.

Patrick
Hamilton
Baskervill,
b. 1848,
(see Basker-
vill Book,
m. Elise⁶
Meade
Skelton
(6-10-1875),
b. 1852.

Dr. John
Gifford
Skelton,
1815-1889,
m. Marianne⁵
O. Meade
(5-7-1846),
b. 1823,
d. 1869.

See Skeltons
of Paxton.

Benj.⁴ L.
Meade,
m. Jane
Elizabeth⁴
Hardaway,
b. 1801.

Genl. Eve-
rard³ Meade,
1746-1802.

Mrs. Mary
Eggleston
Ward,
b. 1759.

Daniel⁵
Hardaway,
b. abt. ——,
m. 1774.

Anne⁵
Eggleston,
b. 1758.

David²
Meade,
m. 1731.

Susanna¹⁵
Everard.

Jos.
Eggleston,
m. 1753;
same as
Anne E.

Judith Segar.

Daniel²
Hardaway,
b. abt. 1715.

Martha
Worsham.

Jos.⁴
Eggleston,
m. 1753.

Judith⁴ Segar
of Middle-
sex,
b. 1729.

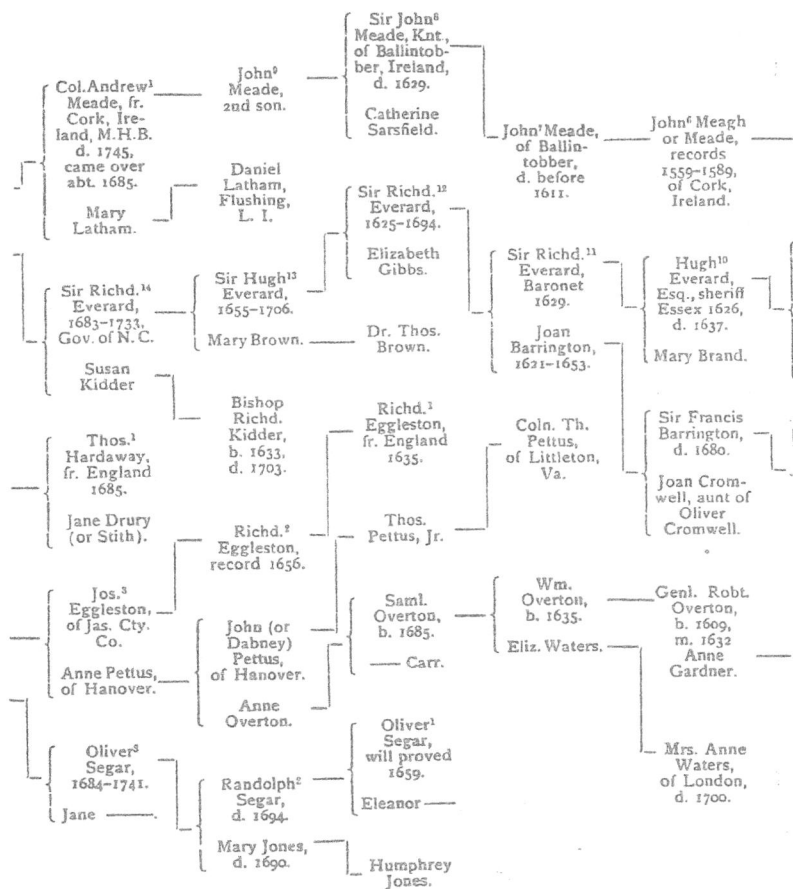

- Col. Andrew[1] Meade, fr. Cork, Ireland, M.H.B. d. 1745, came over abt. 1685.
- Mary Latham.
- Sir Richd.[14] Everard, 1683-1733, Gov. of N.C.
- Susan Kidder
- Thos.[1] Hardaway, fr. England 1685.
- Jane Drury (or Stith).
- Jos.[3] Eggleston, of Jas. Cty. Co.
- Anne Pettus, of Hanover.
- Oliver[3] Segar, 1684-1741.
- Jane ———.

- John[5] Meade, 2nd son.
- Daniel Latham, Flushing, L. I.
- Sir Hugh[13] Everard, 1655-1706.
- Mary Brown.
- Bishop Richd. Kidder, b. 1633, d. 1703.
- Richd.[2] Eggleston, record 1656.
- John (or Dabney) Pettus, of Hanover.
- Anne Overton.
- Randolph[2] Segar, d. 1694.
- Mary Jones, d. 1690.

- Sir John[6] Meade, Knt., of Ballintobber, Ireland, d. 1629.
- Catherine Sarsfield.
- Sir Richd.[12] Everard, 1625-1694.
- Elizabeth Gibbs.
- Dr. Thos. Brown.
- Richd.[1] Eggleston, fr. England 1635.
- Thos. Pettus, Jr.
- Saml. Overton, b. 1685.
- —— Carr.
- Oliver[1] Segar, will proved 1659.
- Eleanor ———
- Humphrey Jones.

- John[7] Meade, of Ballintobber, d. before 1611.
- Sir Richd.[11] Everard, Baronet 1629.
- Joan Barrington, 1621-1653.
- Coln. Th. Pettus, of Littleton, Va.
- Wm. Overton, b. 1635.
- Eliz. Waters.

- John[6] Meagh or Meade, records 1559-1589, of Cork, Ireland.
- Hugh[10] Everard, Esq., sheriff Essex 1626, d. 1637.
- Mary Brand.
- Sir Francis Barrington, d. 1680.
- Joan Cromwell, aunt of Oliver Cromwell.
- Genl. Robt. Overton, b. 1609, m. 1632 Anne Gardner.
- Mrs. Anne Waters, of London, d. 1700.

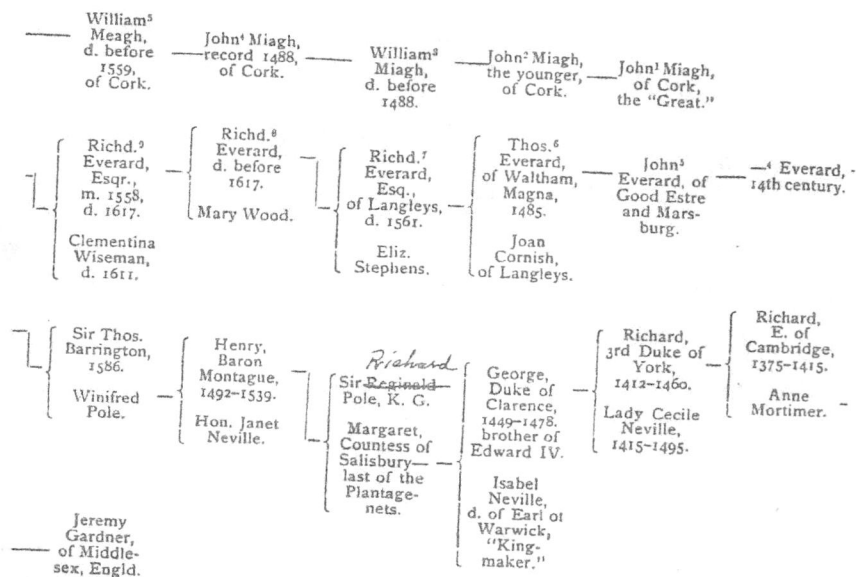

William⁵ Meagh, d. before 1559, of Cork. — John⁴ Miagh, record 1488, of Cork. — William³ Miagh, d. before 1488. — John² Miagh, the younger, of Cork. — John¹ Miagh, of Cork, the "Great."

Richd.⁹ Everard, Esqr., m. 1558, d. 1617.
Clementina Wiseman, d. 1611.

Richd.⁸ Everard, d. before 1617.
Mary Wood.

Richd.⁷ Everard, Esq., of Langleys, d. 1561.
Eliz. Stephens.

Thos.⁶ Everard, of Waltham, Magna, 1485.
Joan Cornish, of Langleys.

John⁵ Everard, of Good Estre and Marsburg.

—⁴ Everard, 14th century.

Sir Thos. Barrington, 1586.
Winifred Pole.

Henry, Baron Montague, 1492-1539.
Hon. Janet Neville.

Richard
Sir ~~Reginald~~ Pole, K. G.
Margaret, Countess of Salisbury— last of the Plantagenets.

George, Duke of Clarence, 1449-1478. brother of Edward IV.
Isabel Neville, d. of Earl of Warwick, "Kingmaker."

Richard, 3rd Duke of York, 1412-1460.
Lady Cecile Neville, 1415-1495.

Richard, E. of Cambridge, 1375-1415.
Anne Mortimer.

Jeremy Gardner, of Middlesex, Engld.

William⁵
Everard,
of Marsburg,
Essex.   ——   Walter²
Everard,
14th century.   ——   Ralph¹
Everard,
13th century.

Roger,
E. of March,
1374–1398.

Lady
Eleanor
Holland.

Edmund,
3rd E. of
March,
1352–1381.

Philippa, of
Clarence.

Lionel
of Antwerp,
Duke of
Clarence,
1338–1368.

Lady Eliz.
de Burgh.

Edward III,
King of
England,
1328–1377.

Philippa, of
Hainault.

THE MEADE FAMILY

MEADE TABLES

THE MEADES IN IRELAND.

1   John[1] Miagh, of co. Cork, called "The Great John Miagh"—was a large land proprietor.

2   John[2] Miagh, "younger."

3   William[3] Miagh, d. before 1488.

4   John[4] Miagh, adjudged in court heir of his father and grandfather Sep. 12, 1488.

5   William[5] Meagh, court record 1559, after his death.

6   John[6] Meagh, Miagh, or Meade. M. P. for city of Cork 1559, and 1585, Recorder, Queen's Attorney, Justice of Province of Munster; died before 1589.

7   John[7] Meade, of Ballintubber, and of city of Cork, deed of settlement Febry. 22nd, 1611.

8   Sir John[8] Meade, Knt. of Ballintubber; Knighted Jany. 23rd, 1623—m. Catherine, d. of Sir Dominick d. Sept. 28, 1629   Sarsfield, Bt., Visct. of Killmallock.

9   Lt. Coln. William[9] Meade of the Irish Brigade, of Ballintubber, b. 1612, m. Elizabeth d. of Sir Robert Graves, Knt. of co. Cork; they had four sons and three daughters.

John[9] Meade, [evidently father of Andrew Meade, emigrant—see p. 16].

a

10

| Sir John Meade, of Ballintobber; b. 1642; d. 1707; Baronet 1703. m. 1-Mary Coppinger, d. s. p. 2-Elizabeth Redman, d. s. p. b— 3-1688, Eliz., d. Viscount Skerrin, M. P. for Dublin. | Robert Meade, of Kinsale, m. Frances, d. of Sir Peter Courthope, Knt. of Little Island—had issue. | Patrick Meade, Brig. Genl., will proven June 30, 1732; d. s. p. | Dominick Meade, (Ven.), b. 1661, Arch-Bishop of Cloyne, m. Mary, d. of Francis Smyth, of Rathcourcy, and had issue. | Elizabeth Meade, m. John Galway, of Lota. | Elianor Meade, m. Godwin Swift, uncle of Dean Swift and Attorney General of Duke of Ormonde. | Katherine Meade, m. William Dunscombe, of Cork. |

b

3rd m.

| | | | | | | |

1 William, d. young.   3 Pierce (Sir) 2nd Bart.—and four daughters.
2 James, d. young.   4 Richard (Sir) 3rd Bart.

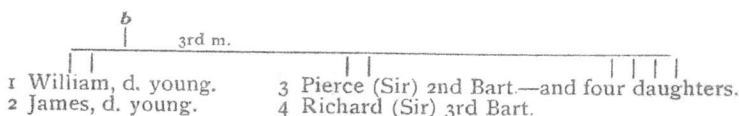

(Note—This being after Andrew Meade came to America, only a skeleton lineage is given.)

10 Sir John[10] Meade, 1st Bart., d. 1711, was succeeded by his son,
11 Sir Pierce[11] Meade, 2nd Bart., d. aged 17, was succeeded by his brother,
11 Sir Richard[11] Meade, 3rd Bart., d. 1744, was succeeded by his son,
12 John[12] (Meade), 1st Earl of Clanwilliam, b. 1744, d. 1800, and was succeeded by his son,
13 Richard[13] (Meade), 2nd Earl of Clanwilliam, d. 1805, s. by his son,
14 Richard[14] (Meade), 3rd Earl of Clanwilliam, d. 1479, s. by his son,
15 Richard[15] James (Meade), 4th Earl of Clanwilliam, d. 1907, s. by his son,
16 Arthur[16] Vesey (Meade), 5th Earl of Clanwilliam, b. 1873—a sitting Member of (English) House of Lords.
     See descriptive sketch, p. 13.

THE MEADE FAMILY OF VIRGINIA.

Emigrant from Ireland about 1685,
first to New York, then to Nansemond county, Va.

a

Andrew¹ Meade, m. Mary Latham,
dau. of Daniel Latham, of Flushing,
Long Island. See p. 27.

seems to have been son of John⁹
Meade of previous table. See p. 16.

Priscilla² Meade, m. Wilson Curle,
of Hampton, Va.—several children.
See E.

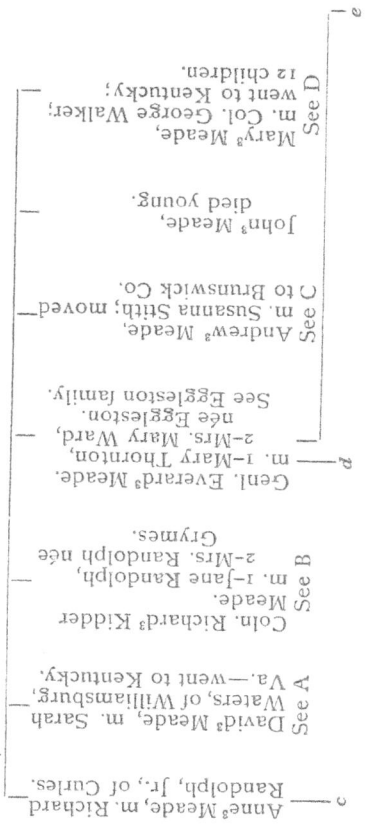

1731
David² Meade, m. Susanna Everard,
dau. of Sir Richard Everard.
See Everard family.

Mary³ Meade,
m. Col. George Walker;
went to Kentucky;
12 children.
See D

John³ Meade,
died young.

Andrew³ Meade,
m. Susanna Stith; moved
to Brunswick Co.
See C

Genl. Everard³ Meade.
m. 1-Mary Thornton,
2-Mrs. Mary Ward,
née Eggleston.
See Eggleston family.

Coln. Richard³ Kidder
Meade.
m. 1-Jane Randolph,
2-Mrs. Randolph née
Grymes.
See B

David³ Meade, m. Sarah
Waters, of Williamsburg,
Va.—went to Kentucky.
See A

Anne³ Meade, m. Richard
Randolph, Jr., of Curles.

e

a

c

NOTE.—The Meade table on pages 5 to 10, beginning with page 6 shows upside down, but this is the correct arrangement. Beginning to read the table on page 5; hold the book sideways with the back from you, and when you turn over to page 6 and the other pages without moving the book, you will find that this arrangement is correct.

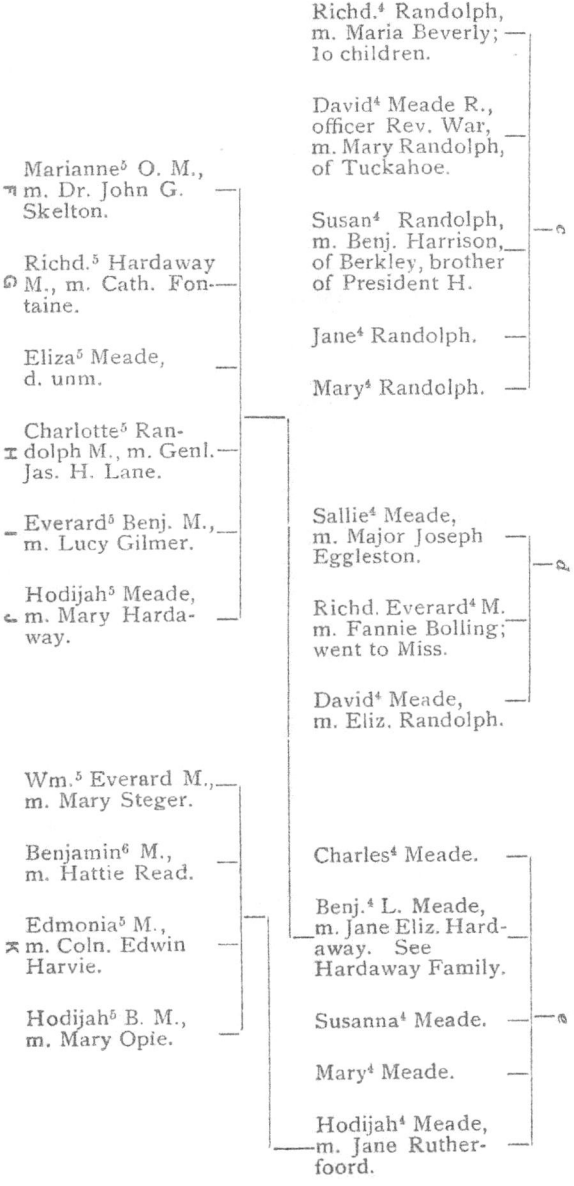

Marianne⁵ O. M.,
m. Dr. John G. —
Skelton.

Richd.⁵ Hardaway
M., m. Cath. Fon-—
taine.

Eliza⁵ Meade,
d. unm.   —

Charlotte⁵ Ran-
dolph M., m. Genl.—
Jas. H. Lane.

Everard⁵ Benj. M.,_
m. Lucy Gilmer.

Hodijah⁵ Meade,
m. Mary Harda- —
way.

Wm.⁵ Everard M.,_
m. Mary Steger.

Benjamin⁶ M.,   —
m. Hattie Read.

Edmonia⁵ M.,
m. Coln. Edwin   —
Harvie.

Hodijah⁵ B. M., _
m. Mary Opie.   —

Richd.⁴ Randolph,
m. Maria Beverly; —
Io children.

David⁴ Meade R.,
officer Rev. War, _
m. Mary Randolph,
of Tuckahoe.

Susan⁴ Randolph,
m. Benj. Harrison,_
of Berkley, brother
of President H.

Jane⁴ Randolph. —

Mary⁴ Randolph. —

Sallie⁴ Meade,
m. Major Joseph —
Eggleston.

Richd. Everard⁴ M.
m. Fannie Bolling;⁻
went to Miss.

David⁴ Meade,   —
m. Eliz. Randolph.

Charles⁴ Meade. —

Benj.⁴ L. Meade,
m. Jane Eliz. Hard-_
away. See
Hardaway Family.

Susanna⁴ Meade. —

Mary⁴ Meade.   —

Hodijah⁴ Meade,
m. Jane Ruther- —
foord.

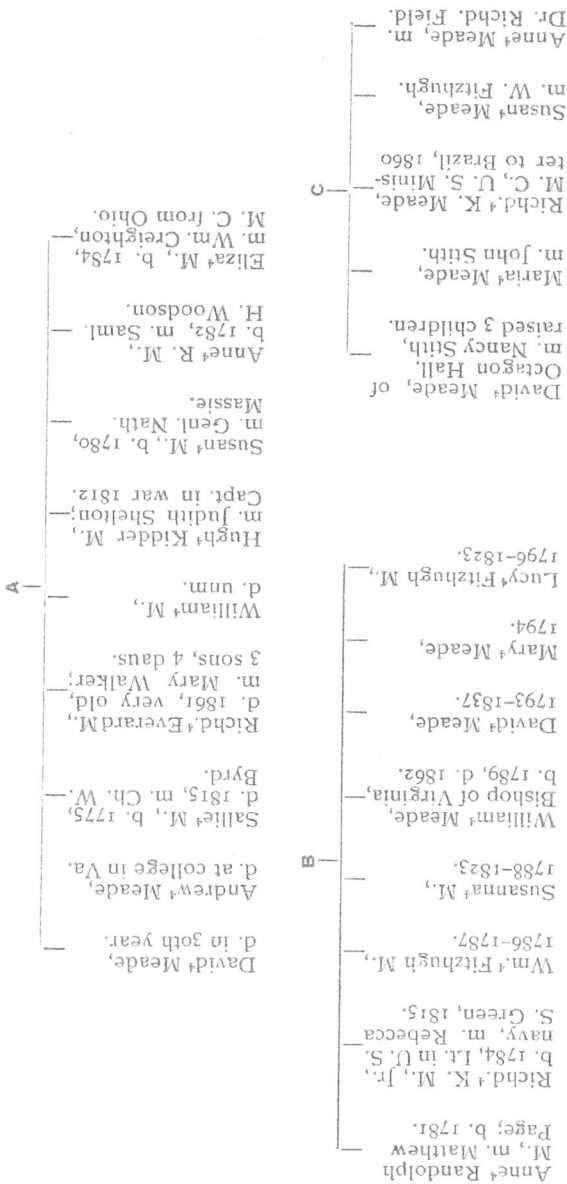

Anne⁴ Meade, m. Dr. Richd. Field.

Susan⁴ Meade, m. W. Fitzhugh.

Richd.⁴ K. Meade, M. C., U. S. Minister to Brazil, 1860

Maria⁴ Meade, m. John Stith.

David⁴ Meade, of Octagon Hall, m. Nancy Stith, raised 3 children.

C

Eliza⁴ M., b. 1784, m. Wm. Creighton, M. C. from Ohio.

Anne⁴ R. M., b. 1782, m. Saml. H. Woodson.

Susan⁴ M., b. 1780, m. Genl. Nath. Massie.

Hugh⁴ Kidder M., m. Judith Shelton; Capt. in war 1812.

William⁴ M., d. unm.

Richd.⁴ Everard M., d. 1861, very old, m. Mary Walker; 3 sons, 4 daus.

Sallie⁴ M., b. 1775, d. 1815, m. Ch. W. Byrd.

Andrew⁴ Meade, d. at college in Va.

David⁴ Meade, d. in 30th year.

A

Lucy⁴ Fitzhugh M., 1796-1823.

Mary⁴ Meade, 1794.

David⁴ Meade, 1793-1837.

William⁴ Meade, Bishop of Virginia, b. 1789, d. 1862.

Susanna⁴ M., 1788-1823.

Wm.⁴ Fitzhugh M., 1786-1787.

Richd.⁴ K. M., Jr., b. 1784, Lt. in U. S. navy, m. Rebecca S. Green, 1815.

Anne⁴ Randolph M., m. Matthew Page; b. 1781.

B

Helen[4] Walker.

Aaron[4] Walker.

Mary[4] Walker.

Jacob[4] Walker.

Courtney[4] Walker.

Susanna[4] Walker.

D—

Walter[5] Walker, killed in Nicaragua.

Jane[3] Curle.

Hamilton[3] Curle.

Mary[3] Curle.

Andrew[3] Curle.

William[3] Curle.

Nicholas[3] Curle.

David[3] Curle.

Wilson[3] Curle.

E—

Mary[4] Curle.

Priscilla[4] Curle.

Julian[6] F. Skelton, b. 1868—unm.

Anne[6] Archer Skelton, 1865, d. 1892, s. p. m. Walter H. Miles.

Marianne[6] E. Skelton, b. 1861, m. Alfred W. Gibbs.

William[6] O. Skelton, b. 1858, d. 1911, unm.

John[6] Gifford Skelton, b. 1855, d. —, m. Lucy S. Landrum.

Benj.[6] Meade Skelton, b. 1853, d. 1879—unm.

Elise[6] Meade Skelton, b. 1852, m. P. H. Baskervill.

Catharine[6] Gifford Skelton, b. 1850, m. Thos. Norman Jones.

Ennion[6] W. Skelton, b. 1848—unm.

Charlotte[6] R. Skelton, b. 1847, m. Llewellyn McVeigh.

F—

Marianne⁷ S. Gibbs, b. 1891,
m. L. Lee Layton.

Frank⁷ Skelton,
m. ———.

Catharine⁷ O. Skelton,
m. Charles Carter.

Maria⁷ Ward Skelton,
m. Wm. Galt.

Landrum⁷ Skelton,
m. ———.

Lucy⁷ S. Skelton,
m. Dr. Thomas White.

John⁷ Gifford Skelton,
m. Catharine Hagan.
b. 1876, d. 1879.

Hamilton⁷ Meade Bas-
kervill, b. 1882.

John⁷ Skelton Baskervill,

Marianne⁷ Gertrude Skel-
ton, m. Corydon Hobson.

Thomas⁷ Norman Jones,
b. 1882,
m. Elsie Wellford.

Catharine⁷ S. Jones,
b. 1874,
m. Wm. Everard Meade.

Carter⁸ Wellford Jones.

Catharine⁸ Jones.

Llewellyn⁷ W. McVeigh,
b. 1870, m. Katharine
Goldsborough.

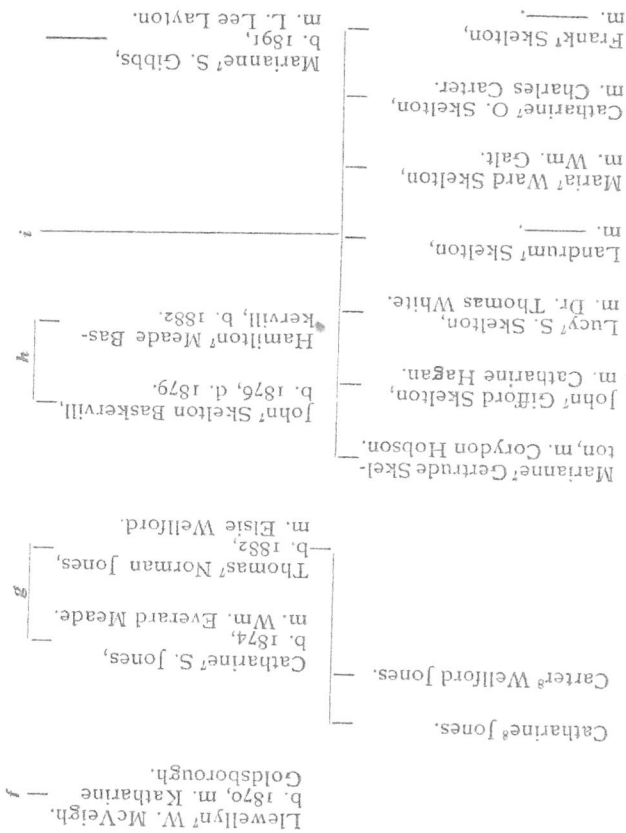

NOTE.—For other names see page 49.
There were nine generations in Ireland before Andrew Meade, hence Hamilton M. Baskerville is (9/7)
16th generation from the beginning.

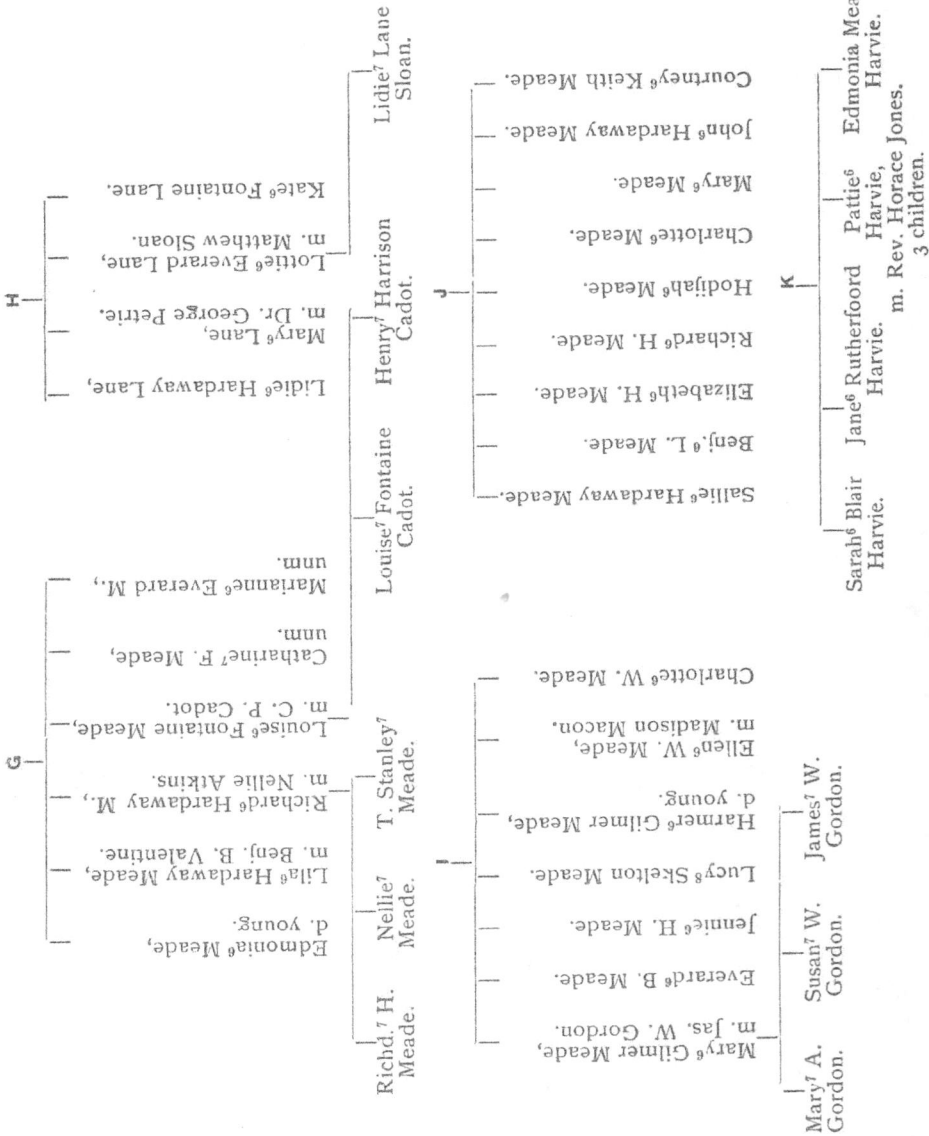

H

- Lidie[7] Lane Sloan.
- Kate[6] Fontaine Lane.
- Lottie[6] Everard Lane, m. Matthew Sloan.
- Mary[6] Lane, m. Dr. George Petrie.
- Lidie[6] Hardaway Lane.
- Henry[7] Harrison Cadot.
- Louise[7] Fontaine Cadot.

G

- Marianne[6] Everard M., unm.
- Catharine[7] F. Meade, unm.
- Louise[6] Fontaine Meade, m. C. P. Cadot.
- Richard[6] Hardaway M., m. Nellie Atkins.
- Lila[6] Hardaway Meade, m. Benj. B. Valentine.
- Edmonia[6] Meade, d. young.
- T. Stanley[7] Meade.
- Nellie[7] Meade.
- Richd.[7] H. Meade.

J

- Courtney[6] Keith Meade.
- John[6] Hardaway Meade.
- Mary[6] Meade.
- Charlotte[6] Meade.
- Hodijah[6] Meade.
- Richard[6] H. Meade.
- Elizabeth[6] H. Meade.
- Benj.[6] L. Meade.
- Sallie[6] Hardaway Meade.

K

- Edmonia Meade Harvie.
- Pattie[6] Harvie, m. Rev. Horace Jones. 3 children.
- Jane[6] Rutherfoord Harvie.
- Sarah[6] Blair Harvie.

- Charlotte[6] W. Meade.
- Ellen[6] W. Meade, m. Madison Macon.
- Harmer[6] Gilmer Meade, d. young.
- Lucy[8] Skelton Meade.
- Jennie[6] H. Meade.
- Everard[6] B. Meade.
- Mary[6] Gilmer Meade, m. Jas. W. Gordon.
- James[7] W. Gordon.
- Susan[7] W. Gordon.
- Mary[7] A. Gordon.

CHAPTER I

THE MEADES IN IRELAND

This book relates of Andrew Meade, of Ireland and Virginia, and *his* ancestors and descendants, and not of the other families of this name, apparently unrelated.

There seem to be a good many sketches of our Meade family of Virginia, but they relate almost exclusively to the modern history in Virginia, and the meagre results of the attempts to trace the family in Ireland seem very full of error.

The writer has adopted the record in the new edition (1912) of Debrett's *Peerage, Baronetage, and Companionage*, prepared and revised by the present Earl of Clanwilliam, the head of the family.

Mr. David Randolph Meade, late of Clarke Co., Va., whose death in July, 1912, is very much to be regretted, had for some years been collecting and preparing material for a book on the Meade family. He wrote for information to the Earl of Clanwilliam, who in March, 1912, with a very kind and cordial letter sent him advance sheets of the Clanwilliam sketch in the new edition of *Debrett's Peerage*, then in press. Mr. Meade kindly sent these to Mrs. Baskervill for inspection and return, and the writer made copies, which we have on file and have recorded here. It is much to be regretted that Mr. Meade did not publish his book before his death.

ANDREW[1] MEADE, the first of the family in this country, who emigrated to America about 1685, and was the ancestor of the Virginia Meades, as shown later, was a member of this Irish family. And although heretofore the connection has not been definitely traced, the relationship is undoubted and is known both here and in Ireland. Now the writer thinks he has discovered a clue, which definitely fixes his parentage, and the definite connection. See page 16.

The name in the older period in Ireland was spelled "Meagh", or "Miagh", and the family lived at Ballintober, or Ballintubber, near Cork, co. Cork, Ireland.

The following is an identical copy of the Earl of Clanwilliam's letter, and a close abstract of the advance sheets of the book:

"Telephone   (coronet)
2219 Kensington.   34 Lowndes Square, S. W.
                                                17. 3. 12.

Dear Mr. Meade:

I enclose two slips of paper, which will give you all the information of the Clanwilliam family that is obtainable.

The Clanwilliam family is one of the oldest families in Ireland, having been settled in the South of Ireland in co. Cork for many generations.

Our home is now in the North of Ireland in county Down— a place called Gillhall, celebrated for the Beresford ghost story, one of the most authentic ghost stories in the world.* I trust these papers may be of some interest and use to you. Please do not return them. We never came from England, and never had anything to do with England.

                            Y. truly,
                                (signed)   Clanwilliam."

The following is taken from the advance sheets for a new edition of *Debrett's Peerage, Baronetage, Knightage and Companionage,* sold from 31s 6d to 50s net, evidently prepared by the Earl of Clanwilliam.

---

* This ghost story may be found in a newspaper clipping in Volume II of our Meade Papers. As it only related to the McGill family, a daughter of which married John Meade, first Earl of Clanwilliam, about 1710, remotely connected with the Virginia Meades, and as it is rather long and tedious, we do not give it here.—P. H. B.

"CLANWILLIAM.

The Earl of Clanwilliam (Sir Arthur Vesey Meade), Viscount Clanwilliam, co. Tipperary, Baron Gillford, of the manor of Gillford, co. Down, in Ireland; Baron Clanwilliam, of Clanwilliam, co. Tipperary, in the United Kingdom; and a Baronet of Ireland; D. L. co. Down; Capt.-gen. Reserve of Officers, late Royal Horse Guards, formerly extra A. D. C. to the Viceroy of India (Lord Curzon of Kedleston), served in S. African War 1900-2 (severely wounded, mentioned in dispatches; b. 14th Jan. 1873; s. his father as 5th Earl in 1907; m. 27th April, 1909, Muriel, widow of Hon. Oliver Howard, and daughter of Russell Stephenson, and has issue:

1. Mary Katherine Selina, b. 16 Febry., 1910;
2. Elizabeth Louise Margaret, b. 18th April, 1911.

Lineage:

This family originally called Meagh, Miagh, and Myagh, have been for centuries settled in the co. and city of Cork, and have been landed proprietors from the earliest mention of the name.

1. JOHN[1] MIAGH, called in Chancery Bills in Ireland "the great John Miagh", was seized in fee of the fishery weir of Lochwacen, in the Haven of Cork. His son;

2. JOHN[2] MIAGH was called the younger and was succeeded by his son;

3. WILLIAM[3] MIAGH, d. before 1488, and was s. by his son;

4. JOHN[4] MIAGH, who was adjudged by a decree or deed of arbitration before Maurice Roche, mayor of Cork, and others, 12 Sept. 4 Henry VII (1488), the weir in the Harbour of Cork, as heir of his father and grandfather. He was succeeded by his son and heir;

5. WILLIAM[5] MEAGH, who is recorded in a Chancery Bill, 4 July, 2 Queen Elizabeth (1559), to have been s. by his son and heir;

6. JOHN[6] MEAGH, MIAGH, or MEADE, was elected M. P. for the city of Cork 1559, and again in 1585. He was recorder of Cork, the Queen's Attorney for Munster, and was appointed

by patent, dated 15 Dec., 1570, second justice of the province
of Munster. He was dead in 1589 and was s. by his son;

7. JOHN[7] MEADE, of Ballintubber, and of the city of Cork.
On 22 Febry., 1611, he made a deed of settlement of his
estates. He was s. by his son;

8. SIR JOHN[8] MEADE, Knt. of Ballintubber, knighted 23rd
Jany., 1623. He m. (settlements dated 22 Febr., 1611) Catherine, dau. of Sir Dominick Sarsfield, Bart., Viscount Killmallock, and had two sons; (1) William[9], his heir; (2) JOHN[9],
see p. 16. Sir John[8] made a deed of settlement of his estates
2 Nov., 1627. He d. 28 Sept., 1629, and was s. by his eldest
son;

9. William[9] Meade, of Ballintubber, lieut. col. in the army,
aged 17 at his father's death. His wardship was granted 11
March, 1632, to Thomas Maule, of Dublin. He m. Elizabeth,
dau. of Sir Robert Travers, Knt., and had with three daughters (1, Elizabeth, m. John Galway, of Lota; 2, Elianor, m.
Godwin Swift, attorney-gen. to the Duke of Ormonde, and
uncle of the celebrated Dean Swift; 3, Katherine, m. Wm.
Demscombe, of Cork) four sons;

1, John (Sir), 1st bart., born in Cork 1642;

2, Robert, of Kinsale, m. Frances, dau. Sir Peter Courthope,
Knt., of the Little Island, and had issue;

3, Patrick, brigadier general, whose will, dated 9th April,
1726, was proved 30th June, 1732, d. s. p.;

4, Dominick (Ven.), b. 1661, archbishop of Cloyne, m.
Mary, dau. of Francis Smyth, of Rathcourcy, and had issue.

Coln. Meade, who raised a troop of horse for the service of
Charles II in 1666, was s. by his eldest son;

Sir John Meade, 1st Bart., and Knt. of Ballintubber, co.
Cork, James of York's attorney general, who was created a
Baronet of Ireland 29 May 1703. Sir John m. 1st Mary, dau.
and heir of James Coppinger; she d. s. p.; he m. 2ndly Elizabeth, dau. and co-heir of Col. Daniel Redman, of Ballyinch
Castle, by whom he had one daughter; he m. 3rdly, 14th June,
1688, Hon. Elizabeth Butler, dau. of Pierce Butler, 2nd Viscount Ikerrin, and by her (who died A. D. 1757) had:

1, William, d. aged 13;

2, James, d. young;

3, Pierce, (Sir), 2nd bart.;

4, Richard, (Sir), 3rd bart.; and four daughters.

(This being after the time of *Andrew¹ Meade's* emigration to America, only a skeleton of the lineage will be copied, especially as the details after this point may be found in *Burke's Peerage** in the Va. State Library).

Sir John Meade, d. 12 Jany., 1711, and was s. by his eldest son;

Sir Pierce Meade, 2nd Bart., d. unm. aged 17, and was s. by his brother;

Sir Richard Meade, 3rd Bart., d. in 1744, and was s. by his son;

John (Meade), 1st Earl of Clanwilliam, b. a few days before his father's death. He d. in 1800, and was s. by his eldest son;

Richard, 2nd E. of C., d. 1805, and was s. by his son;

Richard, 3rd E. of C., d. 1879, and was s. by his son;

Richard James, 4th E. of C., d. 1907, and was s. by his 2nd son,

Arthur Vesey, 5th E. of C.—(see beginning).

Creations—Baronet 29th May, 1703; Baron and Viscount 17 Nov., 1766; Earl 20 July, 1776, all in Ireland; Baron of the United Kingdom 28 Jan. 1828.

Arms—Gules, a chevron, ermine, between three trefoils slipped argent.

Crest; On a wreath of colors, an eagle with two heads displayed sable.

Motto—Toujours prêt.

Seats—Gill Hall, Dromore, co. Down, and Badgemore, Henley-on-Thames, Tocon House, 36 Draycott Place, S. W., Clubs; Turf, Marlborough, and Bachelors.

This lineage from *Debrett's Peerage* is doubtless reliable, as far as it goes, but it includes only the oldest surviving sons, and some of their families. The name of ANDREW¹ MEADE does not appear in it. Mr. Randolph Meade thought he was

* The account in *Burke's Peerage* begins with Sir John¹⁰ Meade, created a baronet in 1703. See page 14.

a brother of John[10] Meade, who was born in 1642 and made a baronet in 1703, and a son of William[9] Meade, of Ballintubber, lieut. colonel in the army. But that was before he had seen the lineage from Debrett, which gives the latter's brothers and sisters, and does not mention ANDREW MEADE, and shows that this is not the correct solution of the matter. The writer thinks he has discovered the true solution, and while it is not absolute, it seems most probable.

SIR JOHN[8] MEADE, mentioned in page 14, who was knighted in 1623, and died in 1629, left two sons,

1, William[9], his heir, who was a lieutenant colonel in the army, &c. See page 14.

2, JOHN[9], of whom nothing more is stated.

Judging from the dates ANDREW[1] MEADE must have belonged to the generation of the children of these two sons. Therefore Mr. Randolph Meade placed him there, but in the wrong family. He is known to have been one of the Meades of Ballintobber, and therefore he must have been of this family. He could not have been a son of William[9] Meade, of Ballintobber, because the names of his sons are given, and he is not among them. Therefore he must have been a son of JOHN[9] MEADE, the younger son of this generation, whose family is not given.

And now we find a confirmation of this in *The Chaumiere Papers*, a family history written by David[3] Meade, grandson of ANDREW[1] MEADE, when he states "He (ANDREW[1] MEADE) had an uncle, Coln. Meade, of the Irish Brigade, a man of much interest at the Court of Versailles". This seems conclusive, and, the writer thinks, definitely settles this long mooted question. We also notice that DAVID[2] MEADE, son of ANDREW[1], named one of his sons John, probably after his grandfather.

A series of articles in regard to the Meades by "Jane Griffith Keys" were published some years ago in the Baltimore *Sun*. She did not have the lineage from Debrett, shown above, and there are some undoubted inaccuracies in her statement; for instance, when she states that ANDREW[1] MEADE was descended from John Meade, 1st Earl of Clanwilliam. Doubtless she got her dates confused, as ANDREW[1] MEADE was a grown man, when he emigrated about 1685; and the earldom of Clanwilliam was not created until 1776, more than a hundred years after he was born. She also mentions William Meade, Bishop of Kildare in 1540 and Privy Councilor to Henry VIII, "whose castle was at Meadestown, co. Cork, Ireland." But he was not an ancestor.

A copy of these articles will be found in our *Meade Papers,* Vol. II.

It is interesting to know that Meades are still living at Ballintobber. From *Armorial Families,* by Fox Davis, 1902, in the Virginia State Library, we get:

"John Josias Meade, Gentleman. Born Sept. 26th, 1858, eldest surviving son of the late John Meade, Esq., J. P., by his wife, Eliza, daughter of Richard Meade, of Dublin. Arms: Gules, a chevron ermine, between three trefoils slipped argent. Crest: On a wreath of colours, an eagle with two heads displayed sable. Motto: Toujours pret. Seats: Ballintobber, Ballinhassig, co. Cork."

"Richard John Meade, Esqr., B. A., J. P., co. Cork, born Apl. 18th, 1865. Arms same as last. Seats: Ballymarble, Kinsale, co. Cork.

"Rt. Rev. Wm. Edwd. Meade, D. D., Dublin, Bishop of Cork, Clyne and Ross. * * * b. Febry. 24, 1832, son of Rev. Wm. Meade, Rector of Inchinabacky. Arms: ecclesiastical."*

The writer has found additional interesting information in regard to the Meades in Ireland in Smith's *History of Cork* in the Virginia State Library. This is an exceedingly inter-

---

*December 8th, 1920.

The previous text was written in 1913, and now it is also interesting to note in regard to the present disturbed condition of Ireland, that the earl of Clanwilliam has sided with the Unionists of Ulster, his residence being as has been stated in county Down. In the Richmond *News Leader* of March 21st, 1914, in an article relating to Ireland, it was stated that Sir Edward Carson, leader of the Unionists, who was staying at the residence of Captain Craig, three miles from Belfast, "continues to hold his 'cabinet councils' with Captain Craig, the marquis of Londonderry, the earl of Ranfurly, *the earl of Clanwilliam,* and other unionist workers."

esting old book, and will well repay a perusal. It was first published in 1750 with the express approval of the Lord Lieutenant of the county, and the Mayor and Council of the city of Cork, and thus became official. And later in 1775 a second edition was published, brought up to date, this copy being of the latter edition published in Cork in 1815. In addition to the text the quaint old illustrations are very interesting. This is a standard history of Cork, and in it are many references to the Meades, of which the following is a summary.

In "a list of mayors of the City of Cork from the earliest to the present time", we find:

1379, David Miagh, Mayor;
1440, John Meagh, Mayor;
1467, John Meagh, Mayor;
1536, Robert Meagh, Mayor;
1548, Patrick Meagh, Mayor;
1555, Christopher Meagh, Mayor;
1570, John Meagh, Mayor;
1595, James Meagh, Mayor;
1600, William Meagh, Mayor;
1601, John Mead, Mayor;
1636, Robert Meagh, Mayor;
1637, David Meagh, Mayor.

Among Protestant mayors and sheriffs 1689, Patrick Mead, Sheriff.

These officers were appointed each year.

Of the Travers family, of whom Elizabeth, d. of Sir Robt. Travers of Co. Cork, married Lt. Coln. William Meade, father of Sir John Meade, 1st Bart., we find:

1731, Robert Travers, Sheriff;
1757, Boyle Travers, Sheriff.

Note Sir Richard Boyle was made 1st Earl of Cork in 1616;
1762, Walter Travers, Sheriff;
1764, Boyle Travers, Mayor;
1776, John Travers, Sheriff.

A mention is made of Meadestown, three or four miles south of Cork, near Carigalene, where stood a castle built by the Meades.

Then we find a mention of Ballintobber, in the parish of Kinsale and near the town of Kinsale, in the barony of Kerry-cuhihy, ten or twelve miles south of Cork, the seat of Sir John Meade, a minor in 1750, whose grandfather was created a baronet by Queen Anne, May 29th, 1703.

The town of Kinsale is on the sea at the mouth of the river Bandon. There are quite a number of castles in the vicinity, some of which remain, and of some the ruins may be seen. "From Inishannon (six miles above), to Kinsale, the river is extremely pleasant, having several houses, castles, and woods on its banks, which are high and beautiful. As one rows down this river, it winds in an agreeable manner, and at the end of each turn the sight is pleasingly entertained with the prospect of some neat seat or romantic building, which open the eye [sic] one after the other." This was in 1750. Ballintobber is on this stretch of six miles, near Kinsale.

Kinsale is an ancient corporation chartered by Edward III in 1333, but the settlement is very much older, as it contained an abbey of "regular canons", of which St. Gobban was abbot in the seventh century. There was also an abbey of Carmelites founded in 1334, of which, part of the ruins still remained in 1750. It is a place of some importance, and has a good harbor. In September, 1601, it was occupied by the Spanish, who held it for several months, but they were finally defeated and evacuated the place on January 2nd, 1602.

An interesting picture of Kinsale is given in the book (*Smith's History of Cork*).

Ballintobber was the ancestral seat of the Meade family, but, we do not find any description of it—only of the surroundings as given above.

The present Earl of Clanwilliam and his family, please remember, now reside at their seat, Gillhall, Dromore, co. Down, Ireland.

The Meades were living also in other parts of the county of Cork. For "On June 3rd, 1749, Mr. Richard Mead (so spelled), of the town of Bantry, at the bottom of the extensive bay of that name, (a good distance East of Ballintobber), to entitle him to a premium given by Rev. Dr. Madden, fully proved to the Dublin Society that he had, within the year, catched and cured 380,000 fish of different kinds, six score to the hundred, a prodigious taking for one man." The expression "six score to the hundred" is curious, and reminds us of the old fashioned "long ton," in which the "quarter" is twenty-eight instead of twenty-five pounds, and "the hundred weight", 112 lbs. instead of 100 lbs.; and so the "baker's dozen" consists of thirteen.

Again we find an interesting description and picture of Butterant Abbey with St. Mary's Chapel (as they were in 1750). In the latter are found "several tombs of the Barrys, the Magners, Fitz-Geralds, Prendergasts, O'Callaghans, Donegans, *Meads*, Dowlings, and Healys". Butterant may be seen on the map in the barony of Kilmore seventeen or eighteen miles N. W. from Cork. It was formerly an ancient corporation, being oncegoverned by a mayor and aldermen, but by the wars gone to decay. There were still to be seen in 1750 the remains of walls that surrounded the town, and also "the remains of a sumptuous ruin of the ancient abbey (just referred to), founded by David de Barry in the reign of Edward I, who (de Barry) lies buried therein. He was Lord Justice of Ireland, and his tomb still remains in the choir, opposite the great altar. The walls of the choir with the nave of the church and several other buildings remain entire; also, the steeple, which is an high square tower erected on a fine Gothic arch; to the South is St. Mary's Chapel, in which are found the tombs referred to." There is much other interesting description too long to find place here. It may be, that these Mead tombs are those of some of the Ballintobber family, or, perhaps, they may belong to another branch of the family.

South of Butterant a short distance is the town of Mallow, which was incorporated by James II on August 29th, 1688, who appointed David Miagh provost, and twenty-six burgesses. It is said, that this town was once reckoned the best village in Ireland. The frequent appointment of the Meades to high office showed their prominence and high standing.

After the death of Queen Elizabeth in 1603 there seems to have been in Ireland a good deal of opposition to acknowledging the accession of James I, and particularly was this the case in Cork. William Mead was "Recorder" and Richard Boyle, afterwards Earl of Cork, was "Clerk to the Council." William Meade seems to have been the leader of the opposition, taking a very earnest and positive stand. The people expressed a doubt as to the death of the Queen, and said they must be satisfied as to that point. They refused to let the King's army into the city, but other citizens opposed this movement and let the army in. And thus the trouble was suppressed.

The present Anglican Bishop of Cork, Cloyne, and Ross, in Ireland, is the Rt. Rev. William Edward Meade, D. D., born in 1832, who was consecrated to that office in 1894. In a letter to Mrs. Baskervill, dated Sept. 14th, 1906, he stated that he was one of the Meades of Ballintober, co. Cork, and was connected with the Virginia Meades. He spelled Ballintober with one b near the end of the word, which is doubtless the modern spelling. His letter is filed in our *"Meade Papers,"* Vol. II.

As stated, we have recorded the detailed history of the lineage only to the death of Sir John[10] Meade, 1st Baronet, who died in 1711, because our ancestor ANDREW[1] MEADE came to America about 1685, and after that our particular interest in the Irish family ceases. A detailed account of the later lineage may be found in any book on the peerage of England, and particularly in *Burke's Peerage*, in the Virginia State Library. Our interest now transfers with ANDREW[1] MEADE to America.

This is all we know of the Meades in Ireland and ends the first chapter of this sketch. We will next take up the Meades in Virginia.

CHAPTER II

THE MEADES IN VIRGINIA

The arms for the Meades in Virginia are the same as for the earls of Clanwilliam, as described on page ~~12~~ *15.*

ANDREW[1] MEADE, of Ballintobber, Co. Cork, Ireland, whose lineage has been given, came over to America about 1685, and was the ancestor of our family of Virginia Meades. Tradition states that he went first to London, and thence came to New York, where he married MARY LATHAM, of Quaker parentage, of Flushing, Long Island, and Bishop Meade in his *Old Churches,* Vol. I, p. 292, states that the Latham family still resided there at that time (1857). The family of MARY LATHAM will be taken up later.

About five years afterwards he removed with his family to Virginia and settled in Nansemond Co., where he became conspicuous and prosperous. He was engaged in trade with the Indians up the Roanoke River, in Virginia and North Carolina, and also in the lumber trade, and became a man of wealth. He built a handsome family mansion and storehouses. The mansion stood on an eminence just back of the town of Suffolk, and had an avenue of trees, which led from it to the church in Suffolk, of which he was a vestryman.

Our information in regard to *Andrew[1] Meade* after his arrival in America is taken to a great extent from two very valuable books written by two of his descendants, viz., *Old Churches and Families of Virginia,* by Bishop William Meade, of Virginia, published in 1857, and *Chaumiére Papers,* containing papers relating to the family, chiefly by David[3] Meade, 1748-1838, of Chaumiére, Kentucky, grandson of Andrew[1] Meade, and edited and published in 1883 by Henry J. Peet, his grandson. While the publication of the former thus preceded by many years that of the latter, the articles contained in the latter had been written many years before, and Bishop Meade tells us that his account "is chiefly taken, even to the letter, from papers found among the relics of the late David[3] Meade, of Kentucky, eldest brother of my father, who lived to be more than ninety years of age, and was much addicted to the study of genealogy." Bishop Meade was a great grandson of ANDREW[1] MEADE through DAVID[2] and Coln. Richard[3] Kidder Meade. Thus we have very good and reliable authority. In addition to these we have other sources of information, among them the first vestry book of the Upper Parish of Suffolk, in Nansemond Co., Va., of which the first record is of November 13th, 1743, two years before the death of ANDREW[1] MEADE.

There are many copies of *"Old Churches,"* including one in our library, but only a few copies of *"Chaumiére Papers"* were printed for private distribution, and they are rare. A friend has lent a copy to the writer for use in preparing this sketch.

David[3] Meade relates of his grandfather: "ANDREW[1] MEADE, my paternal grandfather, was an Irish Catholic, born in the county of Kerry (Ireland). [This is an error. Ballintobber, the seat of the Meade family, is in county Cork, not Kerry. Kerry is west of Cork]. Tradition says he left his native country, and went first to London, and from thence to New York about the latter end of the 17th century. He resided some years in New York, and there married Mary Latham, of Quaker parentage, and some time after he removed to Virginia, and settled permanently at the head of navigation on the Nansemond River.

"It has never been ascertained that he ever formally renounced the Catholic faith, though he was many years a representative of his county in the House of Burgesses, judge of the court, and senior colonel of the militia, executing these offices with advantage to his adopted country, and credit to himself, particularly the two former for which he was eminently qualified by education, which was scholastic, and supposed to have been received either in France or Flanders. He is said to have been a large man, of great corporeal strength, and rather hard featured, but of fine form. In the year 1745 he deceased, leaving a character without stain, having had the glorious epithet connected with his name, long before he died, of 'Honest.'

"Anything further than is above related relative to the origin of my grandfather is chiefly conjecture. * * *

"The Clan William coat of arms is the same as ours. The honors of that house originated in the reign of George II [1727-1760], and I believe not very early in it. * * *

"It is not an improbable hypothesis, that being unfriendly to William the Third's succession to the throne of England, he was forced out of his native country, not unhappily for him, as it appears, as his fortune in America was benign, nor has it been unfortunate for his progeny.

"He left a son, David[2], and a daughter, Priscilla[2], who married Wilson Curle, of Hampton. David[2] Meade, the son, inherited the paternal estate, and about the year 1729 or 1730 married Susannah[15] Everard, the elder of the two daughters of Sir Richard[14] Everard, Bart., of Broomfield Hall, Much Waltham Parish, in the County of Essex, England, and Susannah Kidder, his wife, eldest daughter of Dr. Richard Kidder, Bishop of Bath and Wells.

"My grandfather, Sir Richard[14] Everard, when a young man, was a captain in Queen Anne's army, and it is probable was with Sir George Rooke, admiral of the British fleet, when he took Gibralter." This will be continued later in the Everard sketch.

It may be well to state that Burke in his *Extinct and Dormant Baronetcies* has the remarkable statement that Susanna Everard, daughter of Sir Richard Everard, Governor of N. Carolina, married a Mr. White, a planter of Virginia, which of course is an error.

The first vestry book of the Upper Parish of Suffolk, in Nansemond Co., begins with its first record of a meeting on November 13th, 1743 when there were present Coln. Andrew[1] Meade, Daniel Pugh, and others. We learn from this book that in 1745 David[2] Meade and Daniel Pugh took the places of their fathers in the vestry, Coln. ANDREW[1] MEADE and Coln. Daniel Pugh having died in that year. Rev. Mr. Balfour was the minister, and it is remarkable that in this year he [the minister] was arraigned for drunkenness, swearing, and other vices, and nothing more is heard of him." (*Old Churches I, 289*). It is doubtless true, as his grandson so states, that ANDREW[1] MEADE was brought up a Roman Catholic, but he evidently did not continue in that faith. In New York he married a Quakeress, and later in Virginia he was a member of an Episcopal vestry, and held several public offices, which was not by law allowed to members of the Roman Catholic Church.

It may be well to state that we find some errors in the *"Old Churches,"* for instance in volume I, page 291, where Bishop Meade states that his ancestor, BISHOP KIDDER, was "derived from the EVERARDS OF ESSEX," a rather remarkable case of inadvertence, when he knew perfectly well that BISHOP KIDDER'S daughter, SUSANNAH, married SIR RICHARD EVERARD, father of SUSANNAH EVERARD, who married DAVID[2] MEADE, as will be shown in our sketch of the Everard family. The book is of incalculable value, but has some inaccuracies in it.

There has been some confusion and uncertainty, as to which of the earlier members of the family were members of the House of Burgesses of Virginia. And this is partly due to an error, which has been made in a recent book, supposed to be an authority of last resort. In 1910 the Virginia State Library issued a carefully edited and elaborate edition of *The Journal of the Virginia House of Burgesses* in 13 volumes. The records are copied from the old manuscripts, but rolls of members were included, made up by the editor from the records and other sources. One of the members of the House which held from 1727 to 1734 without dissolution was "Mr. Meade," a representative from Nansemond Co., frequently spoken of in the records. The editor, evidently unfamiliar with the history of the family, has entered the name of the member as "David Meade" both in the rolls and in the index, while in the records, the only old part of the work, he is invariably called "Mr. Meade." The first DAVID[2] MEADE, son of ANDREW[1] MEADE, was born in 1710 or 1711, so that on Febry. 10th, 1727, when he is said to have been present as a member, he was only seventeen years old. Of course this could not have been, and it was undoubtedly ANDREW[1] MEADE, who died in 1745, and not DAVID[2] MEADE, born in 1710, who was a member of this House of Burgesses, which lasted from 1727 to 1734. This same journal shows that David[2] Meade, who was born 1710, and died 1757, was not at any time a member of the House of Burgesses, but that David[3] Meade, son of David[2] Meade, filled this office from Nansemond Co. in 1769. This House of Burgesses, Mr. Meade tells us in *Chaumiére Papers*, was quickly dissolved by Governor Lord Botetourt, and Mr. David[3] Meade did not again seek this office. The journal shows that none of the other Meades of that period were in the House of Burgesses.

We have treated this matter at some length because a loose impression seems to prevail with some of the family that all the Meades of that period were members of the House of Burgesses, and because the high authority of the book mentioned makes it important that for the sake of accuracy this error should be corrected.

The Virginia land books show that on Febry. 22, 1727, ANDREW[1] MEADE patented a tract of 136 acres of land in the Upper Parish of Nansemond Co., and this seems to be the only land grant to a Meade in Virginia.

As stated, ANDREW[1] MEADE married MARY LATHAM, of Flushing, Long Island. Her father was DANIEL LATHAM, who had at least three children:

1. Mary Latham, m. (as stated) ANDREW[1] MEADE;

2. Daniel Latham, Jr., whose descendants are stated by Bishop Meade to have been still residing in Flushing, Long Island, in 1857;

3. Priscilla Latham, m. ———— Hill.

Of the last the issue was as follows:

1. Priscilla Hill, m. J. Montford, four children;
2. Henry Hill, m. ————, three children;
3. Sarah Hill, m. A. McCullough, seven children;
4. Mary Hill, m. Jno. Campbell, two children.

Most of the descendants of Mary Hill are in the West and Northwest. Judge J. L. Bailey and his children, and John Kerr are some remaining in the state (New York?) This statement of the Lathams is from an old memorandum of Wm. O. Skelton, and he says it is from a note on an old family tree.

The Texas Ranger, Ben McCullough, was a descendant of Sarah Hill. In regard to him we get the following from the *Library of Universal Knowledge*, IX, 284: "Ben McCullough, 1814-1862, born in Tennessee, took part in the struggle for Texan independence, and distinguished himself in the Mexican War. In 1853 he was made a United States marshal, and in 1857 commissioner of Utah. He was a brigadier general in the Confederate service during the Civil War, and commanded in several engagements in Missouri. He was killed at the battle of Pea Ridge."

ANDREW[1] AND MARY (LATHAM) MEADE had at least two children;

Priscilla[2], who married Wilson Curle, of Hampton, Va., and had six sons and two daughters; and

DAVID[2], b. 1710, d. 1757, who married SUSANNAH[15], daughter of SIR RICHARD[14] EVERARD, BARONET, Governor of North Carolina (see Everard Family).

Of the former we know little. The names of her children will be found in the table on page 8.

DAVID[2] MEADE, b. 1710, d. 1757, lived at the paternal residence near Suffolk, and died there. In the year 1731 he married, as stated, SUSANNAH[15] EVERARD.

Through the courtesy of Mrs. Lila Meade Valentine, of Richmond, we have been enabled to present pictures of these two ancestors, photographed from portraits belonging to her. These are copies of original portraits belonging to members of the family living in Petersburg, Va.

From the *Chaumiére Papers* we get:

"My father, DAVID[2] MEADE, some time before his marriage made an acquaintance with the family of SIR RICHARD EVERARD, who resided at Edenton, [N. C.], the then seat of government of North Carolina, where an attachment, perfectly

DAVID[2] MEADE, OF NANSEMOND CO., VA.
First of the family born in America; born 1710, died 1757. From a
portrait belonging to Mrs. Lila Meade Valentine, Richmond, Va.

romantic, was mutually formed between my father and the eldest daughter of Sir Richard. * * *

"Having relinquished his government [on Febry. 25, 1731] SIR RICHARD EVERARD AND HIS LADY and two daughters became the guests [by invitation] of my grandfather Meade, he living convenient to Hampton Roads, where the ship lay, in which they had taken their passage to England. From some cause or other the ship was delayed longer than was expected, [partly it is said on account of unfavorable winds], which delay proved favorable to my father's views, who had but little expectation of obtaining the parents' consent to his marriage with their daughter in Virginia, [he being only nineteen years old], and he was preparing to accompany the family to England, when the earnest entreaties of his father, who was distressed at the thought of being so long and so widely separated from his only son, prevailed upon the parents of my mother to consent to an immediate marriage. They, with the most entire confidence in his honor and affection, put their daughter under the protection of her enraptured lover. No pair ever enjoyed more happiness in the hymeneal state than they did. They were both of them very young when they came together, and with very little experience in mankind, brought up under the eyes of fond and virtuous parents.

"My father was of handsome person and fine statue. He lived a monotonous and tranquil life. The purity of his heart corresponded with the symmetry of his person. He was the most affectionate of husbands, the tenderest of parents, and the best of masters, and an ingenuous and sincere friend. Brought up in his father's house, with such a pattern, he could not but be just, generous, and hospitable. If it were thought to detract anything from his merits, it would not be here recorded that he had never studied human nature. Ever disposed to believe men to be what they should be, if he detected an individual deviating from strict probity, he considered him a monster. Venial faults excited in him astonishment, and crime horror. In fine, he was a truly virtuous man, but no philosopher. He deceased in the year 1757, being then in his 47th year."

No apology is needed for giving, substantially in full, this very attractive sketch.

DAVID[2] MEADE succeeded to many of his father's honors. He became vestryman, colonel of militia, and held other offices. He inherited the larger portion of his father's estate including the family seat, and his wife is said to have been heiress to the large estate of her father, SIR RICHD.[14] EVERARD, in England. Her elder brother Richard[15] succeeded to the baronetcy, and became the 5th baronet, but he died unmarried in 1741. He was succeeded by his brother Hugh as 6th baronet. Hugh, however, for some reason was disinherited, and received only the empty baronetcy, while Susannah inherited the property. He went to Georgia and married there, but died without children in 1745. Thus the baronetcy became extinct and the family heritage went to the sister, MRS. SUSANNAH EVERARD MEADE.

This estate is said to have consisted of six manor houses with the estates, viz: Broomfield Hall, co. Essex; Walnut Tree Farm, Copywold Farm, co. Hampshire; freehold of Heathfield, co. Sussex, with a handsome mansion, on what is said to be the precise spot on which the Battle of Hastings was fought by SIR RICHARD EVERARD'S ancestor, WILLIAM THE CONQUEROR; Tower Hill Farm, co. Somerset, near the city of Wells, on which farm SUSANNAH EVERARD'S grandfather, RT. REV. RICHARD KIDDER, Bishop of Bath and Wells, had a fine mansion; and in addition to all this, the London house with all the jewels and furniture thereto pertaining. Langleys, co. Essex, for so many generations the family seat, where the family had been buried, was not included, because SIR RICHARD EVERARD had sold it before going to North Carolina.

In regard to the fine old mansion, the family seat of ANDREW[1] MEADE and DAVID[2] MEADE, in Nansemond Co., Va., near Suffolk, Bishop Meade writes:

"ANDREW[1] MEADE built a large house on this spot for his residence, and storehouses also, as he still carried on trade by a creek which came up almost to his door. The mansion has long since been consumed by fire, and the other houses mouldered into ruins. The estate has passed into many hands

Mrs. David[2] Meade, née Susanna Everard.
From a portrait belonging to Mrs. Lila Meade Valentine, of
Richmond, Va.

since the last of the family parted with it. But there was one spot which it was hoped would be spared until the dissolution of the earth—the grave yard—so well was it guarded. It was a small square lot, around which cedar trees were planted so thick that their bodies reached within one or two feet of each other. A better enclosure, and one more likely to endure, can not well be imagined. I visited the place some years since for the first time [1857 or earlier] and was sorry to find that the last owner of it had cut down every tree and converted them into stakes and firewood. The stumps, however, were perfectly apparent. The grave yard was thickly covered with grass, leaves, briers, and shrubs—so much so that no memorial of the dead was found at first. Later the corner of one slab was all we could see or feel." But all this did not preserve it. Later at Bishop Meade's request a friend went there to inspect and report the condition of the place. "He found not a stump or shrub remaining, but only a number of small fragments of tombstones about the spot, which was in the midst of a cultivated field, itself plowed and cultivated." No fragment with the name could be found. And he adds: "Perhaps no tombstone with that name was ever there, although some of the family must have been buried there." This seems rather a remarkable statement.

Coming back to DAVID[2] MEADE, it is interesting to observe in *Old Churches* that "in 1748 the order for a new church at Suffolk was renewed" (in the vestry)—that it was to be a handsome brick church, and DAVID[2] MEADE and Lemuel Riddick allowed to put up at their own expense galleries for their families.

We also notice that in 1766 Rev. Mr. Lunan, the minister, was presented by the Vestry to Commissary Robinson (for some misconduct), and in the following year David Meade and Thomas Gilchrist were ordered to prosecute the case. But the date shows that this was David[3], the younger.

DAVID[2] MEADE died in 1757 in his 47th year, which shows that his birth occurred about 1710.

DAVID[2] AND SUSANNAH (EVERARD) MEADE had five sons and two daughters:

1. David[3], b. 1744, d. 1838, m. Sarah Waters in 1768;

2. Richard[3] Kidder, aide de camp to Genl. Washington; m. 1st Jane Randolph, of Curles, 2nd Mrs. Randolph, widow of Wm. Randolph, of Chatsworth, formerly Mary Grymes;

3. EVERARD[3], our ancestor, aide de camp to Genl. Lincoln; m. 1st Mary Thornton, 2nd MRS. MARY WARD, widow, née Eggleston;

4. Andrew[3], m. Susanna Stith, of Brunswick Co.;

5. John[3], who died in his youth;

6. Anne[3], m. Richard Randolph, of Curles;

7. Mary[3], m. Coln. Walker, and went to Kentucky.

As we shall see, the three oldest sons were educated in England, at Harrow school, of which the head master at that time was Dr. Thackeray, Arch Deacon of Surry, Chaplain to the Prince of Wales, and grandfather of the great novelist of that name. A current story is that the persons and characters of the three brothers furnished to Wm. M. Thackeray the suggestion of his novel, *The Virginians*.

We find a brief autobiography of David[3] Meade in the *Chaumiére Papers*, of which we may quote at least some items.

"He was born on July 29th, 1744, old style, and his parents determined, as he was a delicate child, to send him to England to be educated, with the hope that his health would be improved. Soon after he had passed his seventh year he embarked in Hampton Roads, under the protection of Mr. John Watson, a particular friend of his father, on board a new schooner, Capt. Bowman. * * * The passage was favorable until the last night the passengers remained on board, when at twelve o'clock, the night being dark and the wind blowing fresh, the schooner struck upon the Goodwin Sands in the channel, and continued to strike with such increased violence that it was expected by all on board that she would every minute go to pieces. * * * The passengers were taken on shore at Deal by boats from that place." Soon after landing "he was seized with a violent fever," of which his parents did not know until after he had recovered. He was sent first to a country boarding school and later to Harrow, where he was "under the care of Rev. Dr. Thackeray, Arch-

Davidᵈ Meade.
Born 1744, died 1830.

THE MEADES IN VIRGINIA

deacon of Surry, and Chaplain to the Prince of Wales, head master of Harrow school." About five years later his next brother, Richard Kidder Meade, arrived at London from Virginia, and joined him at Graham's, a private school, at Dalfton, in Hackney parish, to which he had been transferred. Later they were removed to Fuller's academy in London, and in 1761 David left England and arrived in Virginia in June. He found his two sisters married, Mary to George Walker, and Anne to Richard Randolph. And he left behind him at Dalfton school two brothers, Richard Kidder and EVERARD. This is the first mention of EVERARD, and we are not told when he went over.

Passing over a long description of the interval, we find that on May 12th, 1768, he married Sarah Waters, of Williamsburg, Va., and in 1769 he was elected a member of the House of Burgesses from Nansemond Co. Meanwhile, his father dying in 1757, he had inherited the paternal estate near Suffolk, Nansemond Co., and was living there. In 1774 he purchased 600 A. of land in Prince George Co., Va., including Maycocks, opposite Westover, and removed thither from Suffolk, having "sold to his brother Andrew his patrimonial seat with about 2,000 acres of land, on the west of the creek, and all the rest of the tract on the east side of the town of Suffolk (about the same number of acres), on which were grist and saw mills." Thus we see that the estate of ANDREW[1] MEADE contained at least 4,000 acres.

It is then stated that "of his four brothers, EVERARD, third from himself, married Mary Thornton before he had completed his eighteenth year, Richard Kidder married Elizabeth Randolph, and Andrew at about twenty married Susanna Stith. John died at seventeen, about the year 1771."

Bishop Meade tells us that in 1774 David[3] Meade, on his removal to Maycocks retired from the vestry in Nansemond after a service of twenty-seven years, and Andrew[3] Meade, his brother, was chosen in his room. Hence Andrew must have removed to Brunswick after that time.

David[3] settled at Maycocks, and is said to have been a successful agriculturist, improving and beautifying the place very much. (See Tyler's *Cradle of the Republic,* page 212). He lived there many years and was famous for his hospitality. Another description of the place may be found in the Massachusetts Historical Society Collections, Vol. III, page 90. Here he resided until the summer of 1796, when he "removed to what is now the State of Kentucky, and on July 4th landed from a boat at Limestown, now Maysville, and permanently settled on a small tract of land previously purchased by his eldest son, David[4], at the head of Jessamine Creek, a lateral branch of the Kentucky River, Fayette (now Jessamine) county, being a portion of the former taken from it in 1797." Here he built and established his place "Chaumiére du Prairie," celebrated in the history of Kentucky, as the finest, handsomest, and most elegant home and private residence in the West. He has very little to say of it, himself, but elsewhere we find that it was so prominent that it was located and named on the early maps of Kentucky. It was located nine miles from Lexington, and here he lived for more than thirty years, with his large family of children.

David[3] Meade was thirty years old in 1774, when he established his home at Maycocks (or Maycox), and fifty-two years old in 1796, when he settled "Chaumiére." And as he had spent large sums of money in developing and beautifying Maycocks, so he did at "Chaumiére," except that the expenditure was much greater at "Chaumiére," where he built and established a home that was the wonder of the West. Indeed the tradition is that he was so extravagant and profuse in his expenditures on these places, that they substantially exhausted his large patrimony, as his methods of administration were not financially profitable, and did not tend to the later comfort and welfare of his family.

In *"More Colonial Homesteads,"* by Marion Harland, 1899, page 65 and f., will be found an elaborate description of "Maycox," with a good deal of family history, taken chiefly from *"The Travels of John Francis, Marquis de Chastellux, in North America,"* he being one of the forty members of the French Academy, and Major General in the French army under Count Rochambeau, who in a description of a "dining-

DAVID³ MEADE, OF KENTUCKY; born 1744, d. 1838.
From a portrait belonging to Mr. E. P. Williams, of New York.

day" there gives much other information. "La Chaumiére du Prairie" is the principal subject of the article, and an elaborate description is given. But the limits of this sketch do not permit a summary of this, and we must be contented to state, that the establishment was very extensive, expensive, and elaborate, and that his entertainment there of prominent people was a matter, we may say, of national prominence. "Rev. Meade C. Williams, D. D., of St. Louis, a descendant, records that Mr. (Colonel) David[3] Meade spent three ample inherited fortunes upon the adornment of Maycox, and the homestead in Kentucky" (Marion Harland)."

The Marquis de Chastellux states: "He is so disgusted [at Maycox] with a culture wherein it is necessary to make use of slaves that he is tempted to sell his possessions in Virginia and remove to New England, and it is supposed that this objection to slavery in Virginia induced him to remove to Kentucky."

He was ninety-four years of age, when he died. His oldest son David[4] had died earlier, in his thirtieth year, and his death was a great blow to his father. Everything was to have been left to him—"Chaumiére, paintings, and other works of art, the magnificent silver plate, the trained house-servants and gardeners." "When his will was opened, it was found that he left it with his surviving children, to divide the property as they deemed best. The sole proviso was that Chaumiére should be kept, as he had made it, for three years."

Marion Harland goes on to tell us that in a charming letter from Mrs. Letcher, a grand-daughter, whose parents were Charles Willing Byrd, and his wife Sallie Meade, oldest daughter of David[3] Meade, that "none of the family feeling able to keep up the place, it was thought best to sell it." And everything was sold at auction. "A coarse, vulgar, man bought it, and seemed to do all he could to spoil the place. He filled the beautiful grounds with horses, cattle, sheep, and swine. He felled the trees, cut down the hedges, and committed such vandalism, as had never been heard of in this country. He pulled down some of the prettiest rooms in the house, stored grain in others, and made ruins of all the handsome pleasure-houses, and bridges through the grounds. He only kept the place long enough to destroy it. The next purchaser in 1850 found Chaumiére but a wreck. All that remained [of the house] was the octagon drawing room, and heaps of stone. Even these have been swept away, and all its beauty laid waste."

The article in *More Colonial Homes* is well worth looking up and perusing.

We have given this subject a large space, because it is interesting family history. We can not follow the family farther, but refer to our table for some of the names.

Among some notes in the back of *Chaumiére Papers* by the editor, Henry J. Peet, we find the following: "Tradition says that David[3], of Chaumiére, died at the age of 94, and his wife at the age of 87. This, however, is evidently incorrect. David[3] Meade, as he says himself, was born in 1744. He died in October, 1830. He was therefore but 86 years old, when he died, and his wife was some years his junior, and died a year before him, probably at about 80 years of age."

It is remarkable that David[3] Meade in his family history does not state when his younger brother EVERARD[3] went to England, only that when he (David[3]) left England in 1761, he left his two brothers, Richard[3] and EVERARD[3] there, at Dalfton school. And this seems to be his only mention of EVERARD[3] in England.

David[3] Meade married Sarah Waters, only child of Coln. Wm. Waters, of Williamsburg, Va.

Coln. Richard[3] Kidder Meade at the age of nineteen married Jane Randolph, of Curles, an aunt of John Randolph of Roanoke, who always called him "Uncle Kidder." She lived but a few years, and had several children, all of whom died before the mother. At the commencement of the Revolutionary War he lived at Coggins Point, in Prince George Co., later the residence of Edmund Ruffin. He took great interest in the struggle, and it is said (most probably after the deaths of his wife and children) he sold his James River estate, reserved three thousand dollars for himself, which he placed in the hands of a friend, and distributed the rest among his relatives. Then he offered for military service and was accepted.

Mrs. David³ Meade, née Sarah Waters,
From a portrait belonging to Mr. E. P. Williams, of New York.

At least as early as May, 1777, he was an aide de camp to General Washington with the rank of colonel, which he retained during the war. He was distinguished as a soldier, and highly esteemed by Washington, who greatly appreciated his services. His career at that time is a matter of general history, and no one had a more brilliant one. Campbell, the historian, tells us, that he and his black horse were well known both to the British and American armies. For more details of his history and the names of his children reference is made to Campbell's *History of Virginia,* Bishop John's *Memoirs of Bishop Meade,* and Bishop Meade's *Old Churches.* He was the father of Bishop Meade.

At the close of the war he married the widow of William Randolph, of Chatsworth, near Richmond, and they had eight children, the fifth being Bishop William Meade. He was the ancestor of the Meades of Clarke Co., where he settled after the war, it being then a part of Frederick Co.

From Haywood's pamphlet, p. 10, we get the following interesting statement:

"During the Revolution it was Col. Richd.[3] K. Meade's painful duty to superintend the execution of Maj. André. In recounting that tragic event to Coln. Theodorick Bland, Jr., under date of Oct. 3rd, 1780, he wrote: 'Poor André, the British adjutant general, was executed yesterday; nor did it happen, my dear sir, (though I would not have saved him for the world,) without a tear on my part. You may think this declaration strange, as he was an enemy, until I tell you that he was a rare character. From the time of his capture to his last moment his conduct was such as did honor to the human race. I mean by these words to express all that can be said favorable of a man. The compassion of every man of feeling and sentiment was excited for him beyond our conception. (*Bland Papers,* II, 34)."

Andrew[3] Meade married Susanna Stith, of Brunswick Co., Va., and moved to that county, where he built "Octagon Hall," which was destroyed by fire in 1873. He was the ancestor of the Brunswick Meades. For this family see Capt. C. T. Allen's statement (pamphlet) in our *Meade Papers,* Vol. II.

Before taking up our own branch of the family we think it desirable to give at least a brief sketch of Bishop William[4] Meade, of Virginia, whose prominence and public usefulness was such, and for whom there was such general esteem and veneration, that his memory is an heritage not only of his branch, but of the whole family.

He was the fifth child of Coln. Richard[3] K. Meade and his second wife, formerly the widow of William Randolph, of Curles, born Mary Grymes, and was born on November 11th, 1789. At the age of seventeen he enter Princeton College, and in 1808 a letter from Dr. Smith, President of that institution, to his mother, states: "Your son has just finished his course of college studies with great credit to himself. His talents, his application, his principles and morals are such as may afford a virtuous and affectionate parent the sincerest and purest consolation."

He very soon determined to devote himself to the ministry of the Episcopal Church, under some difficulties, especially the weakness of his eyes, from which he suffered during his whole life.

There being no theological seminary then, he resumed his studies under ministerial supervision, and having followed a course of ecclesiastical studies prescribed by the House of Bishops in 1804, he received Deacon's orders from Bishop Madison on February 24, 1811, and was ordained priest in 1814.

He became rector of Millwood parish in 1821, and was active for many years in promoting the American Colonization Society. Although chosen assistant to Bishop Moore in 1829, he served as rector of Christ Church, Norfolk, for several years, being consecrated Bishop of Virginia in 1841. He was strongly opposed to the Tractarian movement in England, and published in America, at his own expense, the writings of Rev. Wm. Goode, subsequently dean of Ripon.

He was much stirred up by the low condition of religion in Virginia, both in and out of the church, and determined to do what he could to reform it. Chiefly through his influence and that of Rev. Mr. Wilmer, also of Alexandria, Bishop Moore became Bishop of Virginia and did his great work here, being

Rt. Rev. William Meade, D. D.,
Bishop of Virginia 1829-1862. Born 1789, died 1862.

THE HOUSE OF BISHOPS AT RICHMOND, VA., OCT., 1859.
Bishop Meade has an x over him.

consecrated in May, 1814. In 1829 Mr. Meade was elected and consecrated Assistant Bishop of Virginia, and upon the death of Bishop Moore in 1841, he became Bishop of Virginia, and he administered that office until his death in 1862.

The good influence of his ministrations and life within and without the diocese was very great, and the improvement and reforms effected are well known. This mere mention is all that can be made here, and for a better treatment of the subject we refer to the account in the early chapters of Bishop Meade's *Old Churches,* and Bishop Johns' *Memoirs of Bishop Meade.*

Bishop Meade was a first cousin of Mrs. Baskervill's grandfather, Mr. Benjamin[4] L. Meade, of the Hermitage, Amelia Co., Va.

There is an attractive picture of the House of Bishops assembled at Richmond, Va., at the General Convention of October, 1859, about eighteen months before the Confederate War began. This picture has been widely copied and is well known, and the person of Bishop Meade is easily recognized by those familiar with his features. We present a copy of this picture, with the figure of Bishop Meade marked X.

It is hard to exaggerate the great amount of good that has resulted from the efforts and influence and prayers of Bishop Meade and a few co-workers. He was a man of fixed determination and inflexible purpose, and in the providence of God he was permitted to attain to some degree of his high purpose.

GENL. EVERARD³ MEADE, OF "THE HERMITAGE",
Aged 9, born 1746, died 1802.
From a portrait said to be by Sir Joshua Reynolds.

CHAPTER III

THE HERMITAGE MEADES

Now we take up our ancestor, GENERAL EVERARD[3] MEADE, the third son. He was educated in England with his two older brothers at Harrow, as stated, and they seem to have been domesticated in the family of Dr. Thackeray for probably five years. They were much attached to the family, and particularly to Mrs. Thackeray. EVERARD is said to have been only seven years old when he went over. David said that the most affecting event of his whole life was his separation from the Thackerays. Mrs. Thackeray is said to have been a "pious, charitable, and in every way exemplary lady."

A picture of EVERARD[3] MEADE, when nine years old, may be found in *More Colonial Homesteads,* page 72, which is a copy of a portrait of him by Sir Joshua Reynolds, owned by Mr. Everard Meade, of Birmingham, Ala., one of his descendants through his first wife, Mary Thornton. The portrait of David Meade also was painted in England by Thomas Hudson, a copy of which also may be found in *More Colonial Homesteads,* page 70, where the original is said to belong to E. P. Williams, Esqr., of New York. We present copies of these pictures. The boys were very young. In this book David's age is given as eight, and EVERARD's as nine. This may be correct, although David was the oldest, Richard next, and EVERARD youngest, because EVERARD and Richard remained in England several years after David returned [Everard returned from England to Virginia in 1764 (*Chau. Papers*).]

We do not know very much of his personal history.

During the Revolutionary War he was aide-de-camp to Genl. Benjamin Lincoln with the rank of major. From Saf-

fell's Records of the Revolutionary War, pp. 271 and 386, we
find that he was commissioned as captain in the second Virginia regiment on March 8th, 1776, and served to May 1st,
1780, when he was appointed aide-de-camp to Genl. Lincoln
with the rank of major, where he served to near the end of
the war. This was his highest rank in the war. In Heit-
man's *"Officers of the Continental Army, 1775-1783,"* we
find "EVERARD MEADE (Va.) Capt. 2nd Va., 8th March, 1776;
major and aide-de-camp to Genl. Lincoln, 1778, to the close
of the war." After the war he was made Brig. General, and
then Major-General of Militia. In Saffell, p. 504, we find him
as MAJOR EVERARD MEADE in a list of officers, for whose revolutionary services Virginia military land grants were issued
prior to 31st December, 1784. And there is also a record of
a payment to him after the close of the war of salary due him
as MAJOR EVERARD MEADE.

In 1767 he built "The Hermitage" in Amelia Co., Va. An
iron plate now (1910) in the parlor fireplace records this date.
Here he lived after the Revolutionary War and entertained
with great hospitality many distinguished men and women, as
well as relations and friends. Every part of the house is said
to be hand-made, with beautiful carvings on the inside. It
contains twelve rooms, the principal ones finished in wainscoting—mahogany grained and panel work—with cornices
finished in mahogany and gold bronze. It has a reception hall
sixteen feet wide and sixteen feet high, and porches front and
back. The house is on a beautifully shaded lawn, and always
had what was called a rose garden adjoining.

The family grave yard at The Hermitage contains about
twenty graves, among them those of GENL. MEADE[3], his wife
and his son, Hodijah[4] and his wife, lovingly called by many
of her relatives "Aunt Meade."

The inscription upon GENL. EVERARD[3] MEADE's tomb is as
follows:

"Sacred to the memory of MAJOR GENERAL EVERARD MEADE,
who died Sept., 1802, aged 56 years.

"He honorably served his country in war and in peace.

THE HERMITAGE,
Built in 1767, burned down in 1915.

"He was through life conspicuous for magnanimity, probity, generosity, and benevolence.

"When he departed this world, he left no better spirit here.

"Erected in Sept., 1834, by Hodijah Baylies, his friend and fellow aide-de-camp to Maj. Genl. Lincoln in the war of the Revolution, in testimony of his regard and enduring affection."

His son, Hodijah[4], was named after his friend Hodijah Baylies, who erected the tombstone. The house is said to be today (1910) as well preserved as when it was built. It was owned by Mr. Wm. Everard Meade's family until about twenty years ago. For several years it was owned and occupied by Mr. Mills Blair, but he has recently (1914) sold it. It is about thirty miles from Richmond. There are fine carbonate of lithia, iron, and salt springs near the house. When Mr. Blair bought the place, he pulled down the porch, and used the stone steps, as a foundation for his stable.

GENL. EVERARD[3] MEADE was a member of the Virginia Convention of 1788.

December 8th, 1920. Since the above was written, several years ago, The Hermitage has been burned to the ground. From a notice of it in the *Times-Dispatch* of Nov. 2nd, 1915, we learn: "The Hermitage, famous since Revolutionary days as the homeplace of Major General Everard Meade, and the scene of a reputed romance between John Randolph of Roanoke and pretty Maria Ward [the grandmother of Mrs. John L. Williams, formerly Maria Ward Skelton], was destroyed by fire Tuesday afternoon [Oct. 29th, 1915.] The place was sold recently by N. M. Blair to B. F. Smith, who has for some time made his home in Richmond. The origin of the fire has not been determined, the flames appearing first in a portion of the building where no fires had been lighted.

"The Hermitage was one of the best known of the older Virginia mansion houses, and dated from 1767. It has been given a permanent place in history. The interior, known for its elaborate wood carving and rare wainscoting, the products of workmanship and materials that can not be reproduced.

"History records that to the home of Major General Meade came frequently as a visitor his friend, John Randolph of Roanoke. Here, it is said, he met Miss Maria Ward, step-daughter of the general and there developed a romance, which did not turn out as a modern storybook would have had it turn out. Miss Ward preferred someone else to the former statesman, proving that great learning is not always the key to the feminine heart."

"Both Coln. Richard[3] K. Meade and GENL. EVERARD[3] MEADE were original members of the Virginia Society of the Cincinnati." Haywood's pamphlet, p. 10.

GENERAL EVERARD[3] MEADE at a very early age married Mary Thornton, daughter of John Thornton, of North Carolina, and by this marriage had the following children:

1. Sallie[4], m. in 1788 Joseph Eggleston, brother of ANNE EGGLESTON, who married DANIEL HARDAWAY, grand parents of Mrs. Baskervill's mother. See Eggleston Table;

2. Everard[4], (called Richard in the Plantagenet Roll), m. Fannie Bolling. They went to Mississippi, and from them are descended the Mississippi Meades;

3. David[4], m. Elizabeth Randolph.

GENERAL EVERARD[3] MEADE married secondly, on Febry. 5th, 1789, MRS. MARY WARD, widow of Benj. Ward, and daughter of JOSEPH[4] EGGLESTON, and sister of ANNE[5] EGGLESTON, who married DANIEL HARDAWAY, just referred to. See Eggleston Table.

From this marriage he had the following children:

1. Charles[4];

2. BENJAMIN[4] L., m. on July 10th, 1819, JANE ELIZABETH HARDAWAY, our ancestors, (see Hardaway Table, and *William and Mary Quarterly*, XVI, 271);

3. Susanna[4];

4. Mary[4];

5. Hodijah[4], m. Jane Rutherfoord.

Of Charles[4], Susanna[4], and Mary[4] we know nothing except the names, and suppose they died young.

Hodijah[4] Meade and his family lived at the Hermitage, where he had four children, whose names are given in the table, p. 6. Some of his descendants continued to live there until a little more than twenty years ago.

BENJAMIN[4] L. MEADE AND HIS WIFE, our grand parents, lived at their place, called "Castlemont," in Powhatan Co., Va., until 1848 or 1850, when they moved to Richmond, and continued to live there. He died soon after moving and was buried at The Hermitage. She died about 1876, and was buried in Hollywood Cemetery.

Their children were:

1. MARIANNE[5] O., m. DR. JOHN G. SKELTON, his second wife, MRS. BASKERVILL's parents. See Skelton Family;

2. Richard[5] Hardaway Meade, m. Catherine Fontaine. They lived in Richmond and their children are still here;

3. Elizabeth[5] Jane, lived with Richard, and died unmarried;

4. Charlotte[5] Randolph, m. Genl. Jas. H. Lane, and moved to Auburn, Ala.;

5. Everard[5] Benjamin, m. Lucy Gilmer. He and his family lived in Richmond;

6. Hodijah[5], m. Mary Hardaway. He was a lawyer and lived in Amelia Co.

Briefly in general reference to the family we will add that the families have generally been large, and the numbers great and widely scattered.

Through the marriage of Anne[3] Meade to Richard Randolph, of Curles, there are a host of Randolph relations, highly respectable people and some of them conspicuous.

David[3] Meade and his family were conspicuous in Kentucky, and from them have come the "Kentucky Meades," cultivated, intellectual people.

Coln. Richard[3] Kidder Meade established his family in Clarke Co., then Frederick Co., Va., where they have continued, at least some of them. The most distinguished member of this branch was Bishop William Meade, of the Episcopal Diocese of Virginia, whom we have previously mentioned. The family still continue in Clarke Co. and Fauquier.

Andrew[3] Meade, and his wife, Susanna B. Stith, lived in Brunswick Co., of which she was a native, and established the family of Brunswick Meades, who are numerous and of high standing. The Petersburg Meades are a branch of this family.

Then coming down one generation we find that Everard[4] Meade, oldest son of GENERAL EVERARD[3] MEADE, and his wife, Fannie Bolling, went to Mississippi, and established the "Mississippi Meades," several of whom have been pleasantly known to our branch of the family. One of these is Rev. Joseph L. Meade, of the Episcopal Church, who on his way to China as a missionary in 1909 spent some weeks in England, part of the time on a visit to Langleys in Essex, the old Everard family seat, of which he wrote an interesting letter to Mrs. Baskervill, mentioned in our Everard sketch.

In *The Clarence Volume* of *The Plantagenet Roll of the Blood Royall,* by the Marquis of Ruvigny and Raneval, London, T. C. and E. C. Jack, 1905, are nominally included all the descendants of Susanna Everard and David[2] Meade. But some of them are omitted, doubtless from want of information, where no clues were known, or letters were not answered. For instance the descendants of Richard[4] Everard Meade are not mentioned.

Also we have a Meade family tree, containing the names, which were available, but not all of them. This is referred to later and given in our general table.

It is well to mention that there is another large family of Meads in this country, who settled first in Pennsylvania, but a branch of them has been established in Virginia since 1746. A brief history of this family may be found in the *William and Mary Quarterly,* X, 191. They have almost invariably spelled the name without the final e, but a few individuals have used it. The claim has been made by at least one member of it that the families are the same, and that they also "are descended from the Earls of Clanwilliam." The last statement can be made only from ignorance, and the first can not be true, unless some one or more of the Irish Meades went to England before 1600, long before ANDREW[1] MEADE was born.

The following is a summary of the sketch mentioned above, called *"Some of the Meads,"* by G. C. Callahan, of Philadelphia:

Rev. Richard[1] Meade lived at Mursley, Buckinghamshire, England. His son, Rev. Matthew[2] Meade, of Stepney, born 1629, died 1699, had fifteen children, Nathaniel[3], Richard[3], William[3], and others. William[3] married and had issue, John[4], William[4], Robert[4], Samuel[4], Pleasant[4], Sarah[4], and others, who came to America about ——, and settled in Bucks Co., Pa., (just across the Delaware River from Trenton, N. J.) John⁴ married and had two sons. He and his brothers, William⁴ and Samuel⁴, moved about 1746 to Loudoun Co., Va., then a part of Fairfax Co. John⁴ and his family moved to Bedford Co., Va., where he died in 1754, and his son, William⁵, administered on his estate. His brother William⁴ also went to Fairfax Co., and then to Bedford Co., and after seven years returned to Loudoun Co., and died there, and was buried in the Friends' burying ground near Leesburg, Va. He left issue, and there are numerous descendants in Loudoun and other counties in Virginia and elsewhere. The sketch names many other members of this family in Loudoun, Bedford, Charles City, and possible other counties.

This statement is made to show that they are not connected in any way with our ANDREW¹ MEADE, who came from Cork, unless there was a family connection before 1600.

General George Gordon Mead, 1815-72, of the Federal army in the Confederate War, was doubtless of this family.

CHAPTER IV

MEADE GENERAL TABLE

The following table, as stated in the caption, is made from Miss Annie Skelton's tree with the addition of many members of the Clarke Co., Va., branch from a list sent by Mr. D. Randolph Meade, and some other additions made by us, as we happen to know of them. This leaves a large number of unknown members of the family, which we have made no effort to gather.

Our plan is, as each name is recorded, to enumerate all the descendants of that person in order, before passing to another of the same generation. The numbers on the left indicate the number of persons recorded. The columns to the right of these indicate the different generations, and the numbers show the children in each family. The small numbers to the right of each given name indicate the generation.

Descendants of Andrew[1] Meade, of Ireland, and Nansemond Co., Va., emigrant about 1685, from a family tree made by Miss Annie Skelton, of Richmond, Va., in ———, later Mrs. Walter H. Miles, with available additions and corrections:

1	Andrew[1] Meade, from co. Cork, Ireland, abt. 1685, m. Mary Latham; 2 children;		
2		1 David[2], b. 1710, d. 1757, m. Susanna Everard; 5 ch.;	
3			1 Anne[3], m. Rich. Randolph, of Curles; 5 ch.;
4			1 Susanna[4] Randolph, m. Benj. Harrison;
5			2 Jane[4] Randolph;
6			3 Richard[4] Randolph, m. Maria Berkeley;
7			4 David[4] M. Randolph, m. Mary Randolph;
8			5 Mary[4] Randolph;
9			2 David[3], b. 1744, d. 1838, m. Sarah Waters 1768; went to Kty.; 8 ch.;
10			1 David[4], d. in 30th year;

11   2 Andrew⁴, d. at college in Va.;
12   3 Sallie⁴, m. Chas. W. Byrd;
13   4 Richd.⁴ Everard, d. 1861, very old, m. Mary
                Walker; 2 ch.;
14   1 David⁵; 10 children;
15   2 Fannie⁵ F., m. Col. Fisher;
16   5 William⁴, d. unm.;
17   6 Hugh⁴ Kidder, m. Judith Shelton, Capt. in war
                of 1812;
18   7 Susan⁴, b. 1780, m. Genl. Nathl. Massie;
19   8 Anne⁴ R., b. 1782, m. Saml. H. Woodson, 8 ch.;
20   1 Tucker⁵ Woodson, m. Evelyn Byrd, 1874;
                3 ch.;
21   1 Anna⁶ Meade Woodson, m. Dr. R. P.
                    Letcher;
22   1 Margaret⁷ Letcher, m. N. L. Bron-
                        augh;
23   2 Robert⁷ Letcher;
24   2 Jessamine⁶ B. Woodson;
25   3 William⁶ Woodson;
26   2 David⁵ Meade Woodson, 1877;
27   3 Joseph⁵ Woodson;
28   4 Samuel⁵ Woodson, 1881;
29   5 Robert⁵ Woodson;
30   6 Kidder⁵ Woodson;
31   7 Sallie⁵ Woodson, m. Alexr. Waddell;
32   8 Betsy⁵ Woodson;
33   3 Richd.³ Kidder, m. 1st Jane Randolph, 2nd Mrs. Ran-
            dolph, née Grymes; 8 ch.;
34   1 Anne⁴ Randolph, b. 1781, m. Mathew Page;
35   1 Sarah⁵ Page, m. Dr. C. W. Andrews;
36   2 Mary⁵ Page;
37   2 Richard⁴ K., b. 1784, d. 1833, m. Rebecca S.
                Green; 5 ch.;
38   1 Susan⁵ Everard, m. Irvine Hite; 3 ch.;
39   1 Susan⁶ Hite, m. ——— Baker, in Fla.;
40   2 William⁶ Hite, killed in Confed. War;
41   3 Mary⁶ Hite, m. ——— Baker, in Fla.;
42   2 Harriette⁵, m. Jas. M. Hite; 2 ch.;
43   1 Drayton⁶ M. Hite, in Balto.;
44   2 Mattie⁶ Hite, d. 1886;
45   3 William⁵ Washington, 1848, m. 1st Virginia
                Meade, of Benvenue; 2nd, Sal-
                lie Calloway, 1867; 6 ch.;

46   1 Anastasius[6], b. 1850, in Washington, D.
        C., m. Anna Mohun; 2 ch.;
47   1 Virginia[7] Washington, b. 1892;
48   2 Francis[7] Mohun, b. 1897;
49   2 William[6] Kidder, b. 1852, of Tombstone,
        Arizona;
50   3 David[6] Randolph, b. 1854, d. 1912; m. 1st
        Eliz. R. Meade, 1882; 2d Bet-
        tie Crown, d. 1909; 11 ch.;
     1st m.:
51   1 Josephine[7] Sands, b. 1883
52   2 Richard[7] K., b. 1885; 14th U. S.
              Calvary;
53   3 Virginia[7] Washington, b. 1886;
54   4 Annie[7] Bolton, b. 1888;
55   6 Bessie[7] Randolph, b. 1892
     2nd m. 1885:
57   7 Sadie[7] Elizabeth, b. 1896;
58   8 Henrietta[7] Cary, b. 1899;
59   9 Louisa[7] Fairfax, b. 1901;
60   10 Blackburn[7] Crown, b. 1904, d. 1911;
61   11 Mary[7] Lee, b. 1907;
62   4 Lucinda[6] Washington, b. 1856, Washing-
        ton, D. C.;
63   5 Virginia[6] Cary, b. 1858, m. Prof. M. B.
        Allmond; 7 ch.;
64   1 Bessie[7] R. Allmond, d. 1909;
65   2 Marcus[7] Allmond;
66   3 Boyce[7] Allmond;
67   4 Cary[7] Allmond;
68   5 Allen[7] Allmond;
69   6 Evelyn[7] Nelson Allmond;
70   7 Wm.[7] Meade Allmond;
71   6 George[6] Wm., b. 1862, Waco, Texas, m.
        Lucy B. Meade;
72   1 Phillip[7] Nelson;
73   2 Catherine[7] Bolton;
74   4 Drayton[5] G., m. 1855, Annie B. Sands, of
        Brooklyn;
75   1 Maria[6] Courtney, b. 1856;
76   2 Eliz.[6] Anne R., b. 1858, d. 1893;
77   3 Josephine[6] Sands, b. 1860, d. 1882;
78   4 Lucy[6] Bolton, b. 1862;
79   5 Charlotte[6] Congrieve, b. 1864;

80	5	Anne[5] Randolph, m. Hugh Hite;
81		1 Richd.[6] K. Hite, d. 1889;
82		2 Hugh[6] H. Hite, killed in Confed. War;
83		3 Randolph[6] Hite;
84		4 Wm.[6] Meade Hite;
85		5 Lucy[6] T. Hite;
86		6 Lewis[6] B. Hite;
87		7 Ludwell[6] Hite, d. 1876;
88		8 Henry[6] Hite;
89	3	William[4] Fitzhugh, b. 1786, d. 1787;
90	4	Susanna[4] Everard, b. 1788, d. 1823, m. 1809, Wm. Fitzhugh;
91	5	William[4], Bp. of Va., b. 1789, d. 1862; m. 1st Mary Nelson, 2d Tomasia Nelson;
92		1 Phillip[5], m. Fannie Page;
93		1 Tomasia[6];
94		2 Frank[6];
95		3 William[6];
96		4 Rev. Everard[6];
97		5 Phillip[6];
98		6 Henry[6];
99		7 Susanna[6];
100		8 Mary[6] N.;
101		9 Fannie[6] B.;
102		2 Rev. Richd.[5] K., m. 3 times; 1, Harriet L. Hopkins; 2, Brown;
103		1 Rev. William[6] H., m. Pattie Powers;
104		1 Alice[7], m. Robt. Prince;
105		1 Wm.[8] Meade Prince;
106		2 Harriotte[7], m. Robt. Botts;
107		3 Anna[7];
108		4 William[7];
109		5 Phillip[7];
110		6 Powers[7];
111		2 Lucy[6] B.;
112		3 Rev. Francis[6] A., m. Martha B. Mosby;
113		1 Richd.[7] Kidder;
114		2 Robert[7] N.;
115		3 Martha[7];
116		4 Mary[6] Nelson;
117		5 Robert[6] L.;
118		6 Tomasia[6] N.;
119		7 Phillip[6] R.;
120		8 Harriette[6] Lee;

121		9 Margaret[6] M.;
122		10 Richd.[6] K.;
123		11 Elizabeth[6];
124		12 Alexander[6] B., m. Fannie L. Dey;
125		1 Fannie[7] L.;
126		13 Waller[6] H.;
127		14 John[6] Johns;
128	3	Francis[5], m. Mary Burwell;
129		1 Richard[6] Kidder;
130		2 Francis[6] Key;
131		3 Maria[6] S.;
132		4 Phillip[6] N.;
133		5 Louisa[6];
134		6 Tomasia[6];
135		7 William[6];
136	6	David[4], b. 1793, d. 1837, m. Mary Catherine Nelson, of Benvenue;
137		1 Mary[5] Catherine, m. Col. Oliver Funsten;
138		1 Louisa[6] Nelson Funsten, b. 1838, m. Hamilton Fletcher;
139		2 Mary[6] Meade Funsten, b. 1840, m. Jno. Thomas;
140		3 Oliver[6] R. Funsten, b. 1842, m. Lucy Lewis;
141		2 Susan[5] Everard, m. Col. David Funsten;
142		1 Mary[6] Funsten, b. 1844, m. Rev. Benj. Reed, St. Louis;
143		2 Susan[6] Funsten, m. Rev. W. Meade Dame, Balto.;
144		3 Robt.[6] Emmett Funsten, m. Lilly Cook, St. Louis;
145		4 Wm.[6] Fitzhugh Funsten, m. Alice Forbes, St. Louis;
146		5 John[6] Johnson Funsten, m. Minnie Moore, Miss.;
147		6 Cary[6] Funsten, b. 1854, m. Col. Jas. A. Slaughter;
148		7 Lizzie[6] L. Funsten, b. 1856, m. Rev. Edwin Hinks, Balto.;
149		8 Emily[6] Funsten, m. Geo. Ward, Winchester;
150		9 Geo.[6] Meade Funsten, Rev., d. in Atlanta, Ga.;
151		10 David[6] Funsten, d. 1865;
152		11 Richd.[6] K. Funsten;

153		3 Richd.[5] Kidder, m. Jane B. Grymes;
154		1 David[6], b. 1838, m. Mary Johnson;
155		2 Edgar[6] Snowden, b. 1842, m. Lucy Grymes;
156		3 Custis[6] G., b. 1845, m. Lizzie Massey, d. 1914;
157		4 Jane[6] Brokenborough, b. 1847, d. 1885;
158		5 George[6] Carter, b. 1854, m. 1st, Ford; 2d, Martha Grymes;
159		4 John[5] Nelson, of White Hall, m. Bettie Mackey;
160		1 Catherine[6], b. 1851, m. Jas. Wm. Fletcher;
161		2 Louisa[6] Nelson, b. 1853, m. Richey;
162		3 John[6] Mackey, b. 1854, m. Jennie Lakin;
163		5 Virginia[5] Washington, m. Wm. W. Meade;
164		6 Nathl.[5] Burwell, m. 1st, Anastasia Stewart; 2d, Eugenia Turner;
165		7 Wm.[5] Fitzhugh, d. unm., 1887;
166		8 David[5], of Benvenue, m. Nannie Snowden;
167		9 Geo.[5] Wm., d. 1860, m. Sally K. Calloway;
168		7 Mary[4], b. 1794, d. 1868;
169		8 Lucy[4] Fitzhugh, b. 1796, d. 1823;
170		4 Genl. Everard[3], d. 1802, m. 1st, Mary Thornton; 2d, Mrs. Mary Ward, born Eggleston;

1st m.:

171		1 Sallie[4], m. Jos. Eggleston;
172		1 Joseph[5] Eggleston;
173		2 Charles[5] Eggleston;
174		3 William[5] Eggleston;
175		2 Richard[4] E., m. Fannie Bolling;
176		1 Mary[5] E., m. Col. S. Dickens;
177		2 Seignora[5], m. Dr. Smith;
178		3 Thomas[5], m. 1st, Mrs. Winn; 2d, Fannie Eggleston;

1st m.:

179		1 Fannie[6];
180		2 Joseph[6] Lyons;

2d m.:

181		3 William[6];
182		4 Charles[5];
183		5 Harriet[5], m. —— Brown;
184		6 Elizabeth[5], m. —— Grant;
185		1 Henrietta[6] Grant;
186		2 Everard[6] M. Grant;

187	3 Malcolm[6] Grant;
188	4 Virginia[6] Grant, m. Dr. Dabney;
189	5 Fannie[6] Grant, m. P. P. Jones;
190	6 Charles[6] E. Grant;
191	7 Rich.[5] Everard, m. Fannie Smith;
192	1 James[6], m. —— Sessions;
193	1 Cornelia[7] B.;
194	2 Richd.[7] E.;
195	3 Hardeman[7];
196	4 Kate[7] Fontaine;
197	5 Fannie[7] H.;
198	6 Anna[7] H.;
199	7 James[7] T.;
200	8 B. Vaughan[7];
201	2 Thomas[6] Tabb;
202	3 Virginia[6], m. Dr. Dabney;
203	4 Mary[6] G., m. W. B. Jones;
204	1 William[7] B. Jones;
205	2 Virginia[7] A. Jones;
206	3 Henry[7] K. Jones;
207	4 Charles[7] H. Jones;
208	5 Seignora[7] P. Jones;
209	6 James[7] T. Jones;
210	7 Frank[7] Jones;
211	8 Anne[7] Jones;
212	5 Richard[6] E.;
213	6 Fannie[6];
214	8 Virginia[5], m. Geo. Gordon;
215	9 Fannie[5] Tabb, m. Judge Guion, of La.;
216	10 Rebecca[5], m. Peyton Eggleston;
217	11 David[5] K., m. Seignora Eggleston;
218	1 Harriet[6];
219	2 Charles[6];
220	3 Emma[6];
221	12 Mary[5] Elizabeth;
222	3 David[4], m. Eliz. Randolph;
223	1 John[5], m. Rebecca Beverly;
224	1 John[6], C. S. A. 1864;
225	2 Jane[6];
226	3 Eleanor[6], m. Rev. Wm. Platt;
227	1 John[7] Platt;
228	2 Cornelia[7] Platt;
229	4 Charlotte[6], m. Julian Ruffin;
230	1 Julian[7] Ruffin, m. Mary Ruffin;
231	2 Jane[7] Ruffin;

232		3	Bessie[7] Ruffin, m. —— Broadus;
233		4	Edmund[7] Ruffin;
234		5	Rebecca[7] Ruffin, m. H. Christian;
235		5 Elizabeth[6], m. Dr. Callendar, of Scotland;
236			1 Thomas[7] Callendar, m. —— Wills;
237			2 Margaret[7] Callendar;
238			3 Charlotte[7] Callendar, m. Ch. Constable;
239			4 John[7] M. Callendar;
240			5 David[7] Callendar;
241	2 Mary[6] Thornton, d. aged 85;
242	3 Charlotte[5], m. Dr. Stockdell;
243		1 John[6] Stockdell;
244		2 Elizabeth[6] Stockdell, m. Wm. Madison;
245			1 John[7] Madison;
246			2 Eliza[7] Madison, m. Wm. Morrison;
247				1 Elizabeth[8] Morrison;
248				2 Hackley[8] Morrison;
249				3 Hugh[8] Morrison;
250				4 James[8] Morrison;
251			3 William[7] Madison, m. Lucy Wilkes;
252				1 Wilkes[8] Madison;
253				2 John[8] Madison;
254				3 Lucy[8] Madison;
255				4 Elizabeth[8] Madison;
256			4 Richard[7] Madison;
257			5 Robert[7] Madison;
258		3 Mary[6] Thornton Stockdell, m. Wm. Harrison, 1892;
259			1 Charlotte[7] Harrison;
260			2 William[7] Harrison;
261			3 John[7] Harrison;
262			4 Virginia[7] Harrison;
263			5 Nannie[7] Harrison, m. Ed. Harrison;
264				1 Edward[8] Harrison;
265				2 Hugh[8] Harrison;
266			6 Mary[7] Harrison, m. Heath Cabaniss;
267			7 Carter[7] B. Harrison, m. Clara Sweeney;
268			8 Robt.[7] Randolph Harrison, m. Lotchen Poindexter;
269		4 Charlotte[6] Stockdell, m. 1st, E. Randolph; 2d, Wm. Magee;

1st m.:

270	1 Margaret[7] Randolph, m. H. Byrd;
271	1 Robt.[8] M. Byrd;
272	2 Hugh[8] Byrd;
273	3 Kate[8] Byrd;
274	4 Margaret[8] Byrd;
275	5 David[8] Byrd;
276	6 Mary[8] Byrd;
277	7 Charlotte[8] Byrd;
278	8 Henry[8] V. Byrd;
279	9 Edward[8] Byrd;
280	2 Mary[7] Randolph, m. Rev. Gerard Phelps;
281	1 Edwd.[8] R. Phelps;
282	2 Charlotte[8] Phelps;
283	3 William[8] Phelps;
284	4 Everard[8] Phelps;
285	5 Margaret[8] Phelps;
286	6 Fannie[8] Phelps;
287	7 Mary[8] Phelps;
288	8 David[8] Phelps;

2d m.:

289	3 Charlotte[7] Magee;
290	4 Anna[7] Magee;
291	5 Everard[6] Stockdell, m. Louisianna Jones;
292	1 Mary[7] Stockdell, m. Carter Thomlin;
293	1 Louisa[8] Thomlin;
294	2 Charlotte[7] Stockdell;
295	3 Wm.[7] Everard Stockdell;
296	4 Virginia[7] Stockdell;
297	5 Helen[7] Stockdell;
298	6 Ryland[6] Stockdell;
299	7 Anne[6] Stockdell;
300	8 Lucy[6] Stockdell;
301	9 David[6] Stockdell;
302	10 Virginia[6] Stockdell, m. Llewellyn Jones;
303	1 Elizabeth[7] Jones;
304	11 Dr. Hugh[6] Stockdell, m. Kate McPherson;
305	1 Hugh[7] Stockdell;
306	2 John[7] Stockdell;
307	3 McPherson[7] Stockdell;
308	4 Willliam[7] Stockdell;
309	5 Frank[7] Stockdell;

310   4 Anne[5] R. (Meade), m. Jas. Lea;
311   1 David[6] Lea, m. 3 times;
312   2 John[6] Lea;
313   3 Mary[6] Lea;
314   4 Charlotte[6] Lea;
315   5 William[6] Lea;

2d m. (of Genl. Everard[3] Meade):

316   4 Charles[4];
317   5 Benjamin[4], m. Jane E. Hardaway;
318   1 Marianne[5] Old, m. Dr. Jno. G. Skelton;
319   1 Charlotte[6] R. Skelton, m. L. W. McVeigh;
320   1 Llewellyn[7] W. McVeigh, m. Catherine Goldsborough;
321   2 Ennion[6] W. Skelton, in San Francisco;
322   3 Catherine[6] G. Skelton, m. T. Norman Jones;
323   1 Kate[7] S. Jones, m. Wm. E. Meade;
324   2 Th.[7] Norman Jones, m. Eliz. L. Wellford;
325   1 Catherine[8] Jones;
326   2 Carter[8] W. Jones;
327   4 Elise[6] Meade Skelton, m. P. H. Baskervill;
328   1 John[7] Skelton Baskervill, b. 1876, d. 1879;
329   2 Hamilton[7] Meade Baskervill, b. 1882;
330   5 Benj.[6] Meade Skelton;
331   6 John[6] G. Skelton, m. Lucy S. Landrum;
332   1 Gertrude[7] M. Skelton, m. Corydon Hobson; 1 child;
333   1 Gertrude[8] Hobson;
334   2 Jno.[7] Gifford Skelton, m. Catherine Hagan;
335   1 Catherine[8] Skelton;
336   3 Lucy[7] Skelton, m. Dr. Thos White;
337   4 Wm.[7] Landrum Skelton;
338   5 Maria[7] Ward Skelton, m. Wm. Galt;
339   6 Catherine[7] O. Skelton, m. Chas. Carter;
340   7 William[6] Old Skelton, d. 1911, unm.;
342   8 Marianne[6] Everard Skelton, m. Alfred W. Gibbs;
343   1 Marianne[7] S. Gibbs, m. L. Lee Layton;

344	9 Anne[6] Archer Skelton, m. Walter H. Miles;
345	10 Julian[6] F. Skelton;
346	2 Joseph[5];
347	3 Maria[5];
348	4 Martha[5];
349	5 Richd.[5] Hardaway, m. Kate Fontaine;
350	1 Edmonia[6];
351	2 Lila[6], m. Benj. B. Valentine;
352	3 Richard[6] H., m. Nellie Adkins;
353	1 Richard[7];
354	2 Nellie[7];
355	3 Stanley[7];
356	4 Louise[6], m. Clarence Cadot;
357	1 Louise[7] F. Cadot;
358	2 Henry[7] H. Cadot;
359	5 Kate[6];
360	6 Marianne[6];
361	6 Eliza[5], d. unm., 1879;
362	7 Charlotte[5] R., m. Genl. Jas. H. Lane;
363	1 Lidie[6] Lane;
364	2 Kate[6] Lane;
365	3 Mary[6] Lane, m. Geo. Petrie;
366	1 Mary[7] Petrie;
367	4 Charlotte[6] E. Lane, m. Mathew Sloan, Ala.;
368	8 Everard[5] B., m. Lucy Gilmer;
369	1 Mary[6] Gilmer, m. Jas. W. Gordon;
370	1 Susan[7] W. Gordon;
371	2 Elizabeth[7] A. Gordon;
372	3 James[7] W. Gordon;
373	2 Everard[6] B.;
374	3 Jennie[6] H.;
375	4 Lucy[6] S.;
376	5 Harmer[6] G.;
377	6 Ellen[6] W., m. Madison Macon, 1920;
378	7 Charlotte[6];
379	9 Hodijah[5], m. Mary Hardaway;
380	1 Benjamin[6];
381	2 Sallie[6];
382	3 Elizabeth[6];
383	4 John[6];
384	5 Hodijah[6];
385	6 Mary[6];
386	7 Richard[6] H.;

387   6   Susanna[4];

388   7   Mary[4];

389   8   Hodijah[4], m. Jane Rutherfoord;

390   1   William[5] Everard (of the Hermitage), m Mary Steger;

391   1   Peyton[6];

392   2   Jane[6];

393   3   Bettie[6];

394   4   Sarah[6];

395   5   Lottie[6];

396   6   John[6], m. Sallie Edmunds;

397   7   William[6] E., m. Kate Jones;

398   8   Edmonia[6];

399   9   Thomas[6], m. Janet Chalmers;

400   2   Benjamin[5], m. Hattie Read;

401   1   Cabell[6];

402   3   Edmonia[5], m. Col. Edwin Harvie;

403   1   Sarah[6] Harvie;

404   2   Jennie[6] Harvie;

405   3   Pattie[6] Harvie, m. Rev. Horace Jones;

406   1   Jennie[7] Jones, m. Halstead Layton;

407   2   Edwin[7] Jones;

408   4   Edmonia[6] Harvie;

409   4   Dr. Baylies[5], m. Mary Opie;

410   1   Julien[6], m. Bettie Bouldin;

411   1   Edmund[7] B.;

412   2   Edmund[6] B.;

413   3   Eugene[6];

414   4   Randolph[6];

415   5   Andrew[3], m. Susanna Stith, Brunswick Co., Va.;

416   1   David[4], of Octagon Hall, m. Ann Stith;

417   1   Ellen[5], m. Dr. Field;

418   2   Oliver[5], m. ———— Bonner;

419   1   Ellen[6] F., m. ———— Clark;

420   2   David[6];

421   3   Oliver[6];

422   3   Robert[5], m. 1st, ———— Booth; 2d, ———— Ashby; 3d, Taylor Waller;

         2d m.:

423   1   Robert[6], m. ———— Johnson;

424   2   Lucy[6], m. Capt. Allen;

425   1   Robert[7] Allen;

426   2   Ellen[7] Allen, m. Hugh Mays;

427   3   Stuart[7] A. Allen;

428   4   Annie[7] M. Allen;

429   5   Hubert[7] Allen;
430   6   Pattie[7] Allen;
           3d m.:
431   3   Waller[6];
432   4   Elizabeth[6], m. Capt. Allen;
433   1   Lucy[7] Meade Allen;
434   2   Flora[7] Hayes Allen;
435   2   Maria[4], m. Jno. Stith;
436   3   Richard[4] K., (U. S. Minister to Brazil 1860),
                    m. Mary Thornton;
437   1   John[5] N., m. Jane Turnbull;
438   1   Andrew[6];
439   2   Elizabeth[6];
440   3   Theophilus[6];
441   4   David[6];
442   2   Anne[5], m. Dr. Creed Haskins;
443   1   Dr. Richard[6] Haskins, m. 1st, Anne Wel-
                      don; 2d, ——— Thweatt;
             1st m.:
444   1   Creed[7] Haskins, m. Lucy Berkeley;
             2d m.:
445   2   Dr. Carter[7] Haskins, m. Eliza Neb-
                       lett, 1893;
446   1   Bena[8] Haskins;
447   2   Louise[8] T. Haskins;
448   3   Nannie[8] Haskins, m. Wm. McK.
                      Marriott;
449   4   Mary[8] Haskins;
450   5   R. Carter[8] Haskins;
451   3   Meade[7] Haskins;
452   4   Richard[7] Haskins;
453   5   Weldon[7] Haskins, m. ——— Graham;
454   6   Mary[7] Haskins;
455   2   B.[6] M. Haskins;
456   3   Maria[6] Haskins;
457   4   Julia[6] Haskins, m. Robt. Harrison;
458   3   Maria[5], m. Dr. Grammar;
459   4   Richard[5] K., m. Julia Haskins; U. S. Minis-
                    ter to Brazil;
460   1   India[6], m. ——— Pannell;
461   2   India[7] Pannell, m. Rev. Wm. Platt;.
462   2   Julia[6], m. ——— Nichols;
463   3   Susan[6], m. ——— Bolling;
464   4   Richard[6] K.;
465   5   Hugh[6];

466   6 Mary[6];

467   7 Marion[6], m. ———— Osborne;

468   8 Dr. David[6], m. ———— Weeks;

469   5 Dr. Theophilus[5], m. Susan Haskins;

470   6 Susan[5], m. Dr. A. B. Haskins;

471   7 Harriotte[5], m. 1st, ———— Scott; 2d, ————
                      Randolph;

472   8 Indiana[5];

473   9 Marietta[5]; m. 1st, ———— Booth; 2d, ————
                      Friend;

474   10 Amelia[5], m. A. F. Goodwin;

475   1 Albert[6] Goodwin;

476   2 David[6] E. Goodwin, m. ———— Montgomery;

477   3 Maria[6] Goodwin, m. ———— Pannell;

478   4 Mary[6] B. Goodwin, m. ———— Wilson;

479   1 Mary[7] B. Wilson;

480   5 Matilda[6] Goodwin, m. Dr. R. A. Wilkins;

481   6 David[6] Goodwin, m. ———— Wickes;

482   6 John[3], d. young;

483   7 Mary[3], m. Col. Geo. Walker; went to Kentucky;

484   1 Susanna[4] Walker;

485   2 Courtney[4] Walker;

486   3 Jacob[4] Walker;

487   1 Walter[5] Walker, killed in Nicaragua;

488   4 Mary[4] Walker;

489   5 Aaron[4] Walker;

490   6 Helen[4] Walker;

491   2 Priscilla[2], m. Wilson Curle, of Hampton, Va.;

492   1 Wilson[3] Curle;

493.   2 David[3] Curle;

494   1 Priscilla[4] Curle;

495   2 Mary[4] Curle;

496   3 Nicholas[3] Curle;

497   4 William[3] Curle;

498   5 Andrew[3] Curle;

499   6 Mary[3] Curle;

500   7 Hamilton[3] Curle;

501   8 Jane[3] Curle.

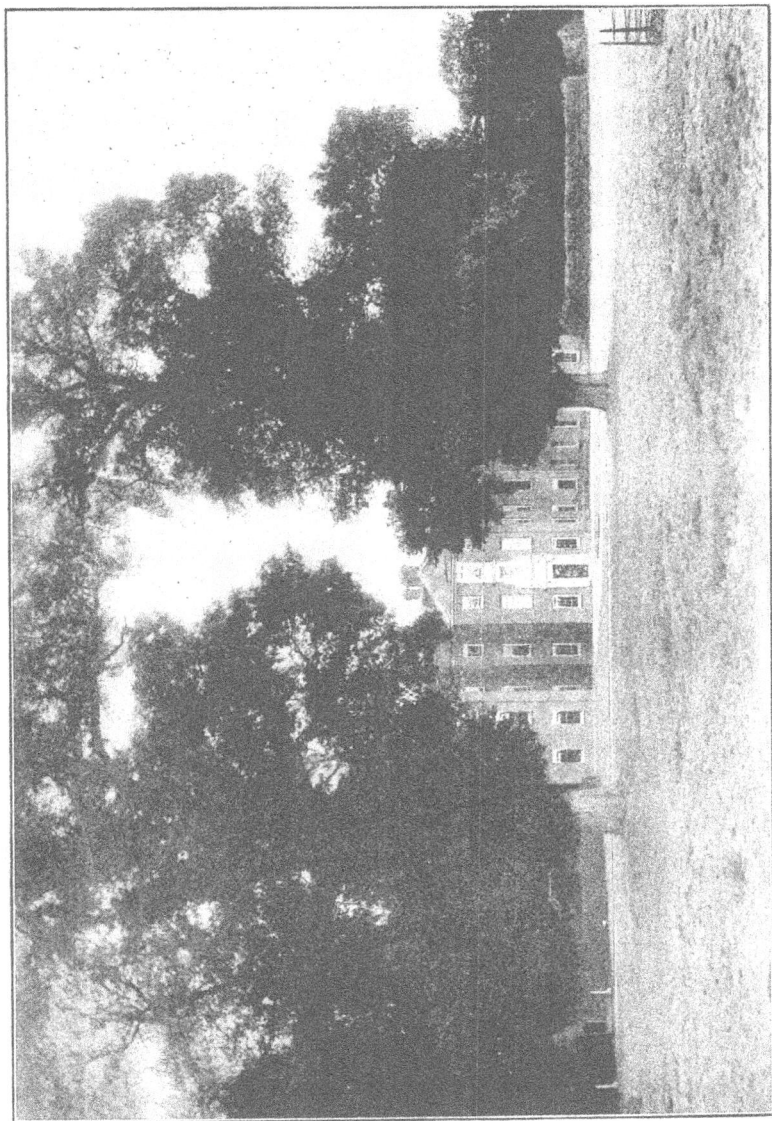

LANGLEYS, CO. ESSEX, ENGLAND.
Seat of the Everard family, front view.

THE EVERARD FAMILY

Everard

CHAPTER V

EVERARD LINEAGE TABLES

THE EVERARD FAMILY TABLE.

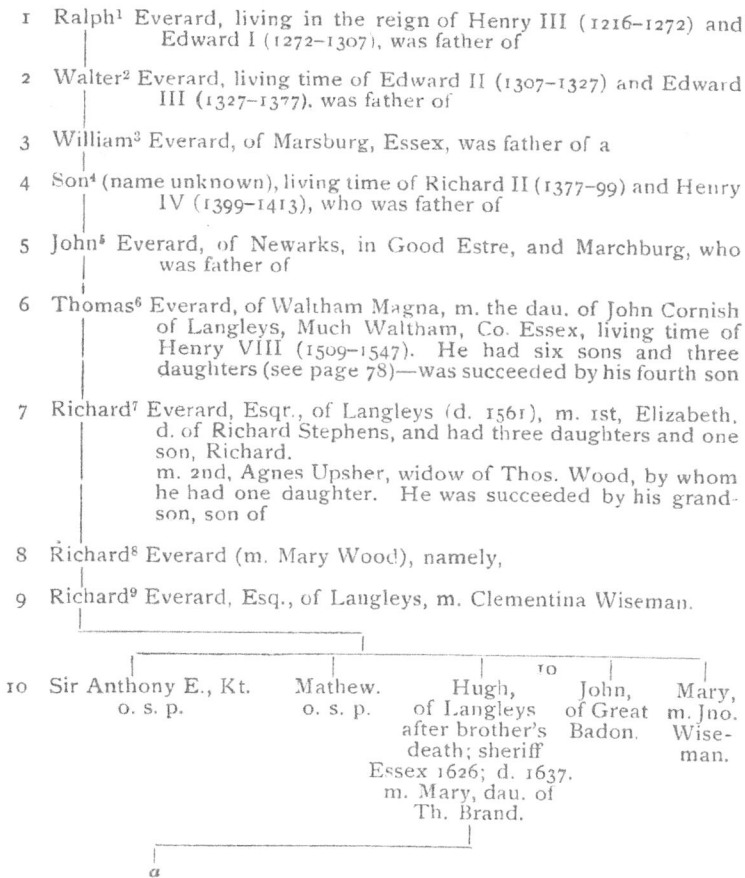

1   Ralph[1] Everard, living in the reign of Henry III (1216–1272) and Edward I (1272–1307), was father of

2   Walter[2] Everard, living time of Edward II (1307–1327) and Edward III (1327–1377), was father of

3   William[3] Everard, of Marsburg, Essex, was father of a

4   Son[4] (name unknown), living time of Richard II (1377–99) and Henry IV (1399–1413), who was father of

5   John[5] Everard, of Newarks, in Good Estre, and Marchburg, who was father of

6   Thomas[6] Everard, of Waltham Magna, m. the dau. of John Cornish of Langleys, Much Waltham, Co. Essex, living time of Henry VIII (1509–1547). He had six sons and three daughters (see page 78)—was succeeded by his fourth son

7   Richard[7] Everard, Esqr., of Langleys (d. 1561), m. 1st, Elizabeth, d. of Richard Stephens, and had three daughters and one son, Richard.
m. 2nd, Agnes Upsher, widow of Thos. Wood, by whom he had one daughter. He was succeeded by his grandson, son of

8   Richard[8] Everard (m. Mary Wood), namely,

9   Richard[9] Everard, Esq., of Langleys, m. Clementina Wiseman.

10 Sir Anthony E., Kt.	Mathew.	Hugh,	John,	Mary,
o. s. p.	o. s. p.	of Langleys	of Great	m. Jno.
		after brother's	Badon.	Wise-
		death; sheriff		man.
		Essex 1626; d. 1637.		
		m. Mary, dau. of		
		Th. Brand.		

a

a

11 Sir Richard[11] E., Bt. 1629, m. 1st, Joan, d. of Sir Fr. Barrington,*
                                            Kt. See tables.
                                    2nd, Frances, dau. of Sir Robt. Lee,
                                            of Billesley.

1st m.

12 Sir Richard E.,   Barrington.   Robert.   Hugh,   Winifred,
        2nd Bt..   o. s. p.   fellow of m. Sir Wm.
    b. 1624, d. 1694,   Emmanuel Luckeyn,
    m. 1, Elizabeth Gibbs,   Cambridge.   Bt.
       2, Jane Finnett.
1st m.

13   Richard E.   Sir Hugh, 3rd Bt.,   Jane,
        died young.   b. 1655, d. 1706,   d. young.
                        m. Mary Brown,
                        buried at Waltham.

14 Sir Richard E., 4th Bt.,   Hugh,   Morton,   Elizabeth,
        d. 1733,   drowned in   killed on   m. Rev. O.
    Gov. of N. Carolina,   storm of   board the   Burne, V. of
    m. Susanna Kidder.   1703.   Hampshire.   Thaxted,
                                                            Essex.

15 Sir Richard E.,   Sir Hugh E.,   Susanna,   Anne,
        5th Bt.,   6th Bt.,   m. David[2] Meade, m. Geo.
    d. unmarried 1741.   d. o. s. p. 1745.   of Va.   Lathbury.
                                          See Meade Family.

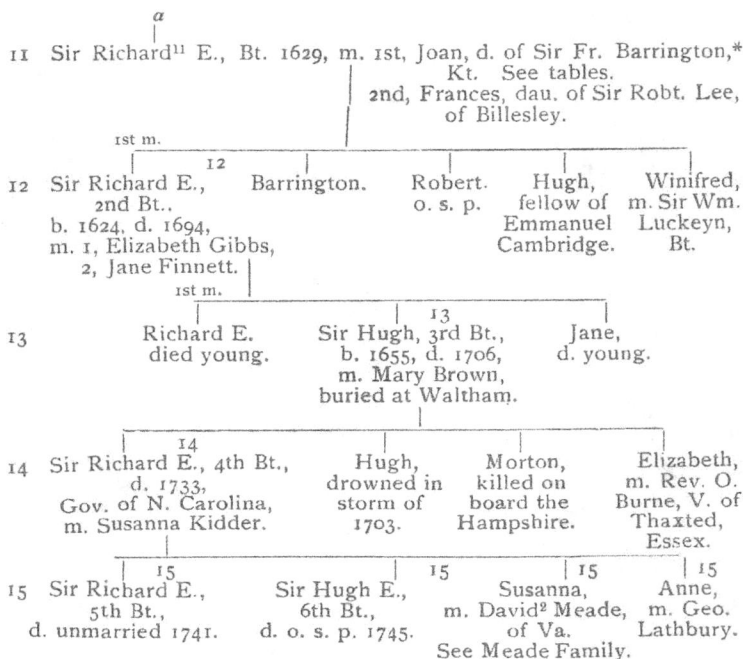

*NOTE.—Through Joan Barrington very interesting lineages are traced
back, royal and otherwise. See page 67 and following.

KING EDWARD III, OF ENGLAND, 1327-1377.
Ancestor of the Everards.

ROYAL DESCENT OF THE EVERARDS, ABBREVIATED

Edward III, Kg. of England, 1328-77; m. Philippa of Hainault;

Lionel, Duke of Clarence, 1338-68; m. Lady Elizabeth Burgh;

Philippa, of Clarence, 1355-82; m. Edmund, 3rd Earl of March;

Roger, E. of March, 1374-98; m. Eleanor Holland;

Anne Mortimer, m. Richard, Earl of Cambridge;

Richard, 3rd Duke of York, 1412-60; m. Lady Cecilia Neville;

George, Duke of Clarence, 1449-78; brother of Edward IV;

Margaret, Countess of Salisbury, m. Sir Reginald Pole, K. G.; b. 1473, last of the Plantagenets; beheaded in Tower, 1541;

Henry, Baron Montague, 1492-1539; m. Hon. Janet Neville;

Winifred Pole, m. Sir Thomas Barrington;

Sir Francis Barrington, 1680; m. Joan Cromwell, aunt of the Protector, see Cromwell table, and Royal Descent table;

Joan Barrington, 1621-1653; m. Sir Richard[11] Everard, Bt.

NOTE—Edward III of England was descended through a line of six kings of England from William the Conqueror, and through his wife, Matilda of Flanders, from Alfred the Great, Charlemagne, and from Hardewick, King of the Saxons, B. C. 90. For full table, see p. 71.

CROMWELL DESCENT.

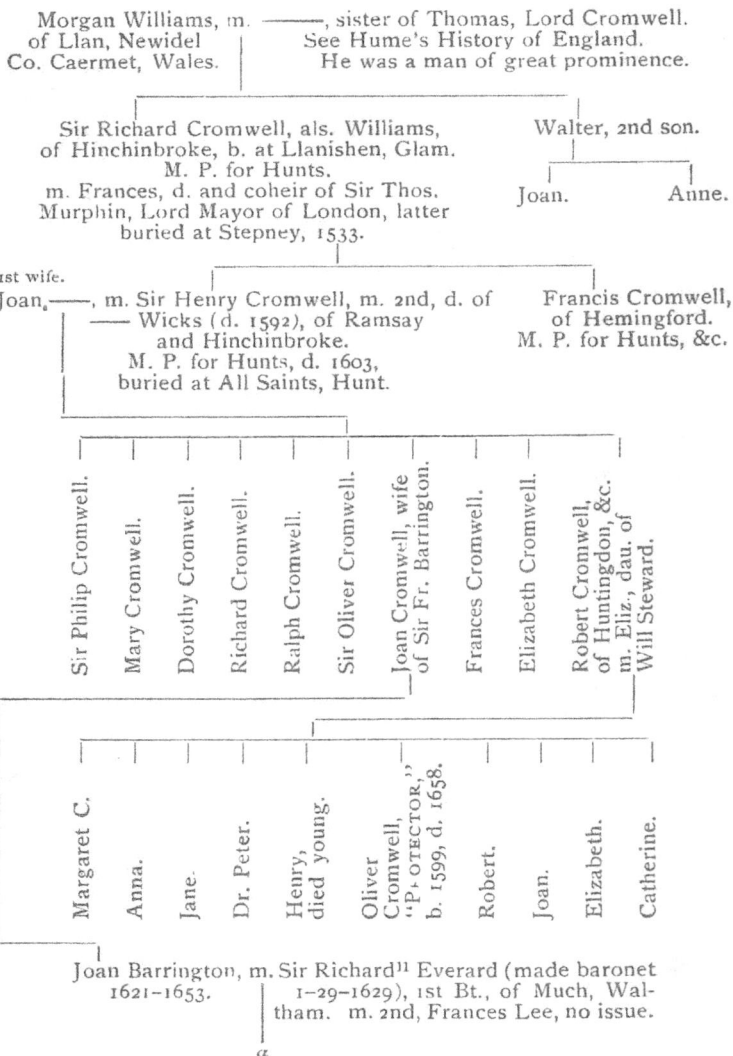

Morgan Williams, m. ————, sister of Thomas, Lord Cromwell.
of Llan, Newidel | See Hume's History of England.
Co. Caermet, Wales. | He was a man of great prominence.

Sir Richard Cromwell, als. Williams,   Walter, 2nd son.
of Hinchinbroke, b. at Llanishen, Glam.
M. P. for Hunts.   Joan.   Anne.
m. Frances, d. and coheir of Sir Thos.
Murphin, Lord Mayor of London, latter
buried at Stepney, 1533.

1st wife.
· Joan,————, m. Sir Henry Cromwell, m. 2nd, d. of   Francis Cromwell,
| ———— Wicks (d. 1592), of Ramsay   of Hemingford.
| and Hinchinbroke.   M. P. for Hunts, &c.
| M. P. for Hunts, d. 1603,
| buried at All Saints, Hunt.

Sir Philip Cromwell.
Mary Cromwell.
Dorothy Cromwell.
Richard Cromwell.
Ralph Cromwell.
Sir Oliver Cromwell.
Joan Cromwell, wife of Sir Fr. Barrington.
Frances Cromwell.
Elizabeth Cromwell.
Robert Cromwell, of Huntingdon, &c. m. Eliz., dau. of Will Steward.

Margaret C.
Anna.
Jane.
Dr. Peter.
Henry, died young.
Oliver Cromwell, "PROTECTOR," b. 1599, d. 1658.
Robert.
Joan.
Elizabeth.
Catherine.

Joan Barrington, m. Sir Richard[11] Everard (made baronet
1621-1653.   1-29-1629), 1st Bt., of Much, Waltham. m. 2nd, Frances Lee, no issue.

a

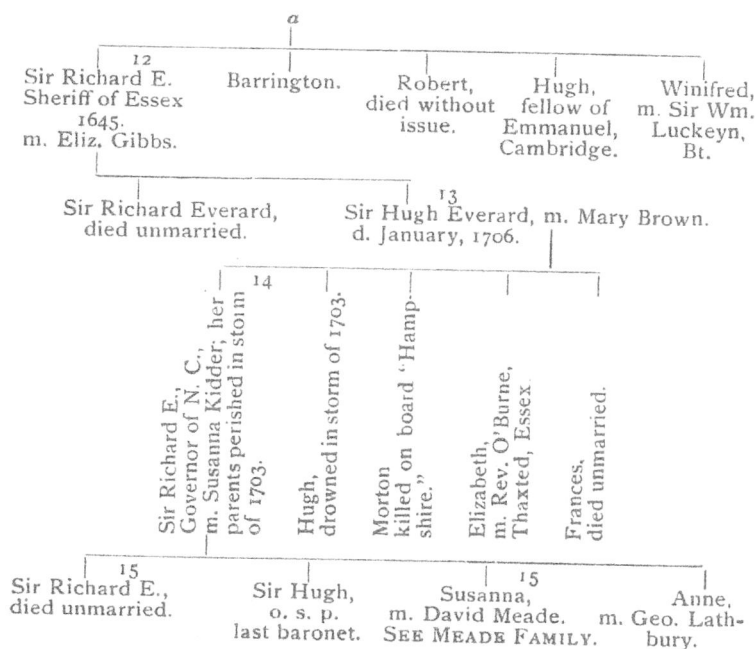

a

12
Sir Richard E.
Sheriff of Essex
1645.
m. Eliz. Gibbs.

Barrington.

Robert,
died without
issue.

Hugh,
fellow of
Emmanuel,
Cambridge.

Winifred,
m. Sir Wm.
Luckeyn,
Bt.

Sir Richard Everard,
died unmarried.

13
Sir Hugh Everard, m. Mary Brown.
d. January, 1706.

14
Sir Richard E.,
Governor of N. C.,
m. Susanna Kidder; her
parents perished in storm
of 1703.

Hugh,
drowned in storm of 1703.

Morton
killed on board "Hamp-
shire."

Elizabeth,
m. Rev. O'Burne,
Thaxted, Essex.

Frances,
died unmarried.

15
Sir Richard E.,
died unmarried.

Sir Hugh,
o. s. p.
last baronet.

15
Susanna,
m. David Meade.
SEE MEADE FAMILY.

Anne,
m. Geo. Lath-
bury.

ROYAL DESCENT OF EVERARDS, RETROSPECTIVE

Table of distinguished and remarkable direct descent through the Everard family, and Joan Barrington, who married Sir Richard[11] Everard. For greater facility and plainness this table being restrospective is reversed, and goes backward. Each person of the list is a son or daughter of the one next below, unless otherwise stated.

1. Hamilton Meade Baskerville;
2. Elise Meade Skelton, m. P. H. Baskervill;
3. Marianne O. Meade, m. Dr. Jno. G. Skelton;
4. Benjamin L. Meade, m. Jane E. Hardaway;
5. Genl. Everard Meade, m. Mrs. Mary Eggleston Ward;
6. Susanna Everard[15], m. David[2] Meade;
7. Sir Richard[14] Everard, m. Susanna Kidder;
8. Sir Hugh[13] Everard, m. Mary Brown;
9. Sir Richard[12] Everard, m. Elizabeth Gibbs;
10. Joan Barrington, 1621-53, m. Sir Rich.[11] Everard;

11. Sir Francis Barrington, 1680, m. Joan Cromwell; see Cromwell Table;

12. Winifred Pole, m. Sir Thomas Barrington; see Barrington Family, p. 95;

13. Henry Pole, Lord Montague, 1492-1539;

14. Margaret Plantagenet, Countess of Salisbury, m. Sir Richard Pole, see Pole Family, p. 95;

15. George Plantagenet, Duke of Clarence, brother of Edward IV, and Richard III, Kings of England, 1449-78;

16. Richard Plantagenet, D. of York, 1412-60;

17. Anne Mortimer, m. [18]Richard Plantagenet, Duke of York, both of these descendants of King Edward III;

18. Roger Mortimer, Earl March, m. Eleanor Holland;

19. Phillipa Plantagenet, m. Edmund Mortimer, Earl of March, 1355-82. See Mortimer Family, p. 97;

[19]Edward Plantagenet, D. of York.

20. Lionel Plantagenet, D. of Clarence, m. Lady Elizabeth de Burgh, 1338-68;

[20]Edmund Plantagenet, D. of York.

21. Edward[a] III (Plantagenet), King of England, 1328-77, m. Phillipa, of Hainault;

22. Edward II (Pl.), 1307-27, m. Isabella, of France, dau. of Philip IV, of France. See table, p. 72;

23. Edward I (Pl.), 1272-1307, m. 1st Eleanor, dau. of Ferdinand, of Castile;

24. Henry III (Pl.), 1216-72, m. Eleanor, of Provence;

25. John (Kg.) (Pl.), 1199-1216;

26. Henry II (Pl.), 1154-89, m. Eleanor, of Guienne;

27. Matilda, m. Geoffrey Plantagenet, Count of Anjou, France;

28. Henry I, 1100-35, m. Matilda, dau. of Malcolm III, of Scotland, see table, p. 72;

29. William I, the Conqueror, 1035-87, m. Matilda, dau. of Baldwin V, of Flanders, traces back to Alfred the Great, see table, p. 73;

30. Robert, 6th Duke of Normandy, 1028-35;

31. Richard III, 5th Duke of Normandy, 1026-28;

32. Richard II, 4th Duke of Normandy, 996-1026;

34. Richard I, 3rd Duke of Normandy, 942-46;

35. William, 2nd Duke of Normandy, 917-42;

---

[a] Here an interesting relationship is found. Richard Plantagenet(16), the younger, was descended from King Edward III through two of his (King Edward's) sons; first through Lionel Plantagenet(20), Phillipa Plantagenet(19), and Roger Mortimer(18) to Anne Mortimer(17), mother of Richard Plantagenet(16); and secondly through Edmund Plantagenet(20), and Edward Plantagenet(19) to Richard Plantagenet(18), father of Richard Plantagenet(16).

36. Rollo, or Robert, the Dane, 1st Duke of Normandy, 911-917, his father was [37]Rognwald, one of the Vikings, Earl of Orkney and Shetland Islands, also Danish King of Dublin, and later Rollo was called "King of Northumberland," and "a rover." This Rollo conquered Normandy and married Gisela, dau. of Charles, the Simple, of France, but she had no children, his two children, William, his successor, and a daughter, being the children of a former wife.

SUPPLEMENTARY LINES

CAPETIAN KINGS OF FRANCE

22. Isabella, of France, dau. of Philip IV, wife of Edward II, of England;
23. Philip IV, of France, 1286-1314;
24. Philip III, of France, 1270-86;
25. Louis IX, of France, 1226-70;
26. Louis VIII, of France, 1223-26;
27. Philip II, of France, 1180-1223;
28. Louis VII, of France, 1137-80;
29. Louis VI, of France, the Fat, 1108-37;
30. Philip I, of France, 1060-1108;
31. Henry I, of France, 1031-60; m. Anne of Russia;
32. Robert II, of France, 996-1031;
33. HUGH CAPET, of France, 956-96, 1st of line;
34. Hugh, the Great, Duke of France, 956;
35. Robert, Count of Paris.

KINGS OF SCOTLAND

28. Matilda, dau. of Malcolm III, of Scotland, and his wife Margaret, of England (see table, p. 74), m. Henry I of England, see p. 71;
29. Malcolm III, Canmore, of Scotland, 1058-93; m. Margaret, of England;

30. Duncan, of Scotland, 1034-40;
31. Malcolm II, of Scotland, 1005-34;
32. Kenneth II, of Scotland, 971-95;
33. Malcolm I, of Scotland, 943-54;
34. Donald, of Scotland, 889-900;
35. Constantine I, of Scotland, 863-77;
36. KENNETH MCALPINE, of Scotland, 844-60; founder of monarchy;
37. Alpine, his father.

COUNTS OF FLANDERS

29. Matilda, dau. of Baldwin V, Count of Flanders, married William, the Conqueror, see p. 71;
30. Baldwin V, Ct. of Fl., d. 1067; m. ———, dau. of Robert, Kg. of France, of the Capetian line, and thus we have another connection here with that line;
31. Baldwin IV, Ct. of Fl., d. 1036;
32. Arnulf II, Ct. of Fl., d. 989;
33. Baldwin III, Ct. of Fl., d. 961;
34. Arnulf I, Ct. of Fl.;
35. Baldwin II, Ct. of Fl., d. 918; m. Aelthryth, daughter of ALFRED THE GREAT, of England, with whom there are two connections, one here, and one through Matilda, of Scotland, wife of Heny I, of England, see 100.
36. Baldwin I, Ct. of Fl., d. 879; m. Judith, dau. of Charles, the Bald, of France, and thus we have another connection with the Carlovingian Kings of France. She was widow of Ethelwolf, Saxon Kg. of England, father of Alfred, the Great (his stepmother)—Baldwin took her by force;
37. Audacer, (may have been same as Baldwin I);
38. Ingelram;
39. Liederic, le Buc, d. 836;
40. Saluart, Prince of Dijon.

THE SAXON KINGS OF ENGLAND

Matilda, of Flanders, dau. of Baldwin V, whose lineage has been given, married William, the Conqueror, and was descended from ALFRED, THE GREAT, through Aelthryth, his daughter, as stated; see Counts of Flanders. Also

28. Matilda, of Scotland, was also descended from him through her mother, Margaret, of England, thus;

29. Margaret, fled to Scotland with her brother after the battle of Hastings; m. Malcolm III, of Scotland;

30. Edward, fled to Hungary during Canute's reign, and married an Hungarian princess, the mother of Margaret;

31. Edmund II, Ironside, Kg. of England, 1016-17;

32. Ethelred II, the Unready, Kg. of England, 978-1016; m. Emma, dau. of Richard I, of Normandy and Gunnora, his wife;

33. Edgar, Kg. of England, 959-75;

34. Edmund I, Kg. of England, 941-48;

35. Edward, the Elder, Kg. of England, 900-25;

36. ALFRED, THE GREAT, Kg. of England, 872-900; said to be the greatest man of all the English kings;

37. Ethelwolf, Kg. of England, 838-857;

38. Egbert, 1st King of all England, 800-838.

NOTE—Back to this point the tracing is plain and easy, and the history authentic and reliable. Farther back we get into difficult ground, and we will adopt the statement of John Anderson, the famous genealogist, in his *"Royal Genealogies"*. Starting with King Egbert, and tracing back, his father was

39. Alchmond;
40. Esa (or Easa);
41. Eoppa;
42. Ingils (or Ingisil), brother to King Ina;
43. Cenred (or Kenred);
44. Ceolwald, (or Chelewald);

45. Cuth (or Cutha) ;

46. Cuthwin, slain in battle against Ardan, Kg. of Scots, in 581 ;

47. Ceolin (or Cheolin) A. D. 560;

48. Chenrick (or Kenrick), "Monarch of the Englishmen", 534;

49. Cherdick (or Cerdick), came to Britain in 495, king in 519; patriarch of the Kings of West Saxons, of whom Egbert, the last, was first monarch of all England;

50. Eliseus ;

51. Esla ;

52. Esla ;

53. Gerisius (or Gerwisch) ;

54. Wigga ;

55. Friaivin (or Frewin) ;

56. Freodegarus (or Frewin) ;

57. Brandius (or Brando) ;

58. Bealdeagus (or Beldeg) ;

59. Bodo (or Woden). He was their deified Mars, and reigned 44 years, 256 to 300 A. D.;

60. Marbod, King of the Saxons, reigned 66 years, 190 to 256;

61. Wilke II, Prince of the Saxons, A. D. 190;

62. Whitekind, King of the Saxons, flourished in 106;

63. Sigwood, Prince of the Saxons, 80 to 100;

64. Svarticke II, Prince of the Saxons, 76 to 80;

65. Svarticke I, Prince of the Saxons, 30 to 76;

66. Wilke I, King of the Saxons, 8 to 30, reigned about the time that Christ was crucified;

67. Anserich, King of the Saxons, A. D. 1, A. M. 4004;

68. Harderich, King of the Saxons, B. C. 90, A. M. 3914.

Merely as a matter of curiosity, which may amuse some of our readers, we will mention that *The Saxon Chronicle* traces this lineage back from Alfred the Great to Adam, the first man. We can take this up in our last table, beginning at Bodo, or Woden, No. 59, thus:

59. Woden;
60. Frithuwald;
61. Freaivine;
62. Fenn;
63. Godwolf;
64. Geat;
65. Taetva;
66. Beaw;
67. Sceldeva;
68. Heremod;
69. Itermon;
70. Hathra;
71. Hwala;

72. Belwig;
73. Sceaf, born in the Ark;
74. Noah;
75. Lamech;
76. Methusalem;
77. Enoch;
78. Jared;
79. Malalahel;
80. Cainion;
81. Enos;
82. Seth;
83. Adam.

This *Saxon Chronicle* seems to be the earliest and most authentic account of Saxon history. One of its contributors was Alfred the Great, and this lineage is said to have been contributed by him.

CHAPTER VI
EVERARDS OF LANGLEYS

DAVID[2] MEADE, of Nansemond Co., Va., in 1731 married SUSANNA[15] EVERARD, daughter of SIR RICHARD[14] EVERARD, 4th Baronet, Governor of North Carolina.

The Everard family is of very old and honorable record, and their seat for many generations was "Langleys", at Much Waltham or Waltham Magna, near Chelmsford, co. Essex, England. They trace back their descent in direct male line to the time of Henry III (1216-1272), and through a lateral line to George, Duke of Clarence, back to two sons of Edward III, of England, and through him to long lines of princes and kings. This will be more fully treated later. We take up first the direct male line.

The following lineage is from Burke's *Extinct and Dormant Baronetcies*, the Baronetcy having been created on 20th Jany., 1628-9, and becoming extinct in 1745.

LINEAGE

1. RALPH EVERARD, living in the reign of Henry III (1216-1272) and of Edward I (1272-1307), was father of

2. WALTER EVERARD, living temp. Edward II (1307-1327) and Edward III (1327-1377), who left a son

3. WILLIAM EVERARD, of Marsbury, in Essex, living in time of Edwards II and III, whose

4. SON and heir was living there in the reigns of Richard II (1377-1399), and Henry IV (1399-1413). He (the son) had two sons, both baptized "John", of whom

5. JOHN EVERARD, the elder, was of Newarks in Good Estre and Marchburg. He left two daughters, Elizabeth and Joan, and a son and heir

6. THOMAS EVERARD, of Waltham Magna, who married JOAN, the daughter and co-heir of JOHN CORNISH, of Langleys, in Much Waltham, county of Essex, and thus became sole owner of Langleys, see page 83. He had six sons and three daughters. From Morant's *Essex* we find that the six sons were (1) John[7], o. s. p.; (2) Thomas[7], m. ———; (3) William[7]; (4) RICHARD[7] (see later); (5) John[7], o. s. p.; (6) Edward[7]. Morant gives their families and also states that Richard[7] Everard, the successor to his father, possessed Langleys, Capons, Whites, Dudborrow, Wardfield, Christianacre, Woodfield, the Herste, Hidemeade, Weights, and many other lands. Coming back to Burke's statement we find that Thomas[6] Everard was succeeded by his 4th son

7. RICHARD EVERARD, ESQR., of the manor of Langleys, in Much Waltham. He married 1st ELIZABETH, daughter of RICHARD STEPHENS, Gent., and had with three daughters an only son [8] RICHARD. He married 2nd Agnes Upsher, relict of Thomas Wood, and by her he had another daughter. He possessed the manor of Langleys, the manor of Havering in Felsted, and several lands and tenements in Little Raine, Little Dunmore, Good Estre, and High Estre, with lands and tenements in Great Waltham. These places may be found on a map in Coller's *The Peoples History of Essex,* in our library. He died 29th December, 1561, and was succeeded by his grandson (son of RICHARD[8] *and* MARY (WOOD) EVERARD), on whom and his heirs by will dated 19th Dec., 1561, he settled the manors of Langleys and Havering.

9. RICHARD EVERARD, Esqr., of Langleys, son of Richard[8] Everard, by Mary Wood, his wife, daughter of Thomas Wood, of Raine Parva. This gentleman married Clementina, daughter of John Wiseman, Esqr., of Great Canfield, and had issue:

(1) Anthony Everard (Sir), his heir;

(2) Matthew Everard, died without issue;

10. (3) HUGH, heir to Much Waltham at the decease of his eldest brother;

(4) John, of Great Badon;

(5) Mary, m. to Jno. Wiseman, Esqr.

This Richard[9] and his wife lived together fifty-three years (she died in Sept., 1611, and he on 25th July, 1617), and lie buried in Waltham Church. He was succeeded by his eldest son Sir Anthony Everard, who received the honor of knighthood 23rd July, 1603, before the coronation of James I. He married 1st Anne, daughter of Sir Thomas Bernadiston, Knight of Ketton, in Suffolk, by whom he left an only daughter and heir, Anne Everard, who married Sir Wm. Maynard, baronet, of Little Easton, afterwards created Lord Maynard (see Burke's *Peerage and Baronetage*), and carried lands in Foxheath and several other parishes, with the lordship of Landon, out of the family. Sir Anthony Everard married 2nd Anne, daughter of Sir Anthony Felton, K. B., of Playford, in Suffolk, but had no children. He died in 1614, was buried at Waltham, and was succeeded by his brother

10. Hugh Everard, Esqr., of Much Waltham, who was Sheriff of Essex, in 1626. He married Mary, daughter of Thomas Brand, otherwise Bond, gent., and dying in 1637 (his wife died the same year, and both were buried in Waltham Church) was succeeded by his only son

11. Richard Everard, Esqr., who was created a baronet by King Charles I on 29th January, 1628-9. Sir Richard married 1st Joan, daughter of Sir Francis Barrington, Baronet, (see Barrington Family, page 99), and had issue:

(1) Richard, his heir;

(2) Barrington;

(3) Robert, died without issue;

(4) Hugh, fellow of Emmanual College, Cambridge; and three daughters, one of whom

(5) Winifred married Sir Wm. Luckyn, Baronet, of Little Waltham Hall; and the other two were

(6) Joan and

(7) Frances, one of whom married Jno. Cutts, Esqr., of Arkden.

He married secondly Frances, daughter of Sir Robert Lee, of Billesley, in the county of Warwick, relict of Sir Gervase Elives, Knt., of Woodford, in Essex, but had no issue. He was succeeded at his decease by his eldest son

12. SIR RICHARD EVERARD, 2nd Baronet, who was Sheriff of Essex in the 20th (year) of Charles I. He married 1st ELIZABETH, daughter of SIR HENRY GIBBS, of Falkland, in Scotland, Knight of the Bedchamber to King James I, and had issue:

(1) Richard, died unmarried;

(2) HUGH, his heir;

(3) Jane, died young.

SIR RICHARD[12], married 2nd Jane, daughter of Sir John Finnet, master of ceremonies to James I and Charles I. He died in August, 1694, aged 70 years, and was succeeded by his son

13. SIR HUGH[13] EVERARD, 3rd Baronet, a military man, who in his early life had distinguished himself in Flanders. He married MARY, daughter of JOHN BROWN, M. D., of Salisbury, and had issue:

(1) RICHARD, his successor;

(2) Hugh, drowned in the great storm of 1703. He was a lieutenant of the Restoration;

(3) Morton, killed on board the Hampshire, commanded by Lord Maynard;

(4) Elizabeth, married to Rev. Mr. O'Burne, vicar of Thaxted, in Essex;

(5) Frances, died unmarried.

SIR HUGH[13] was Receiver General of the land tax, and Justice of Peace for the county of Essex. He died in January, 1705-6, aged 51, was buried at Waltham, and was succeeded by his son

14. SIR RICHARD[14] EVERARD, 4th Baronet, who married SUSANNA, daughter and co-heir of DR. RICHARD KIDDER, D. D., BISHOP OF BATH AND WELLS, (his lordship [with his wife] was killed at his palace in Wells by the great storm in November, 1703), and had issue:

(1) Richard, his heir;

(2) Hugh, heir to his brother;

15. (3) SUSANNA, m. in Virginia (1731) DAVID[2] MEADE;

(4) Anne, m. George Lathbury (Betham's Baronetage I, 369).

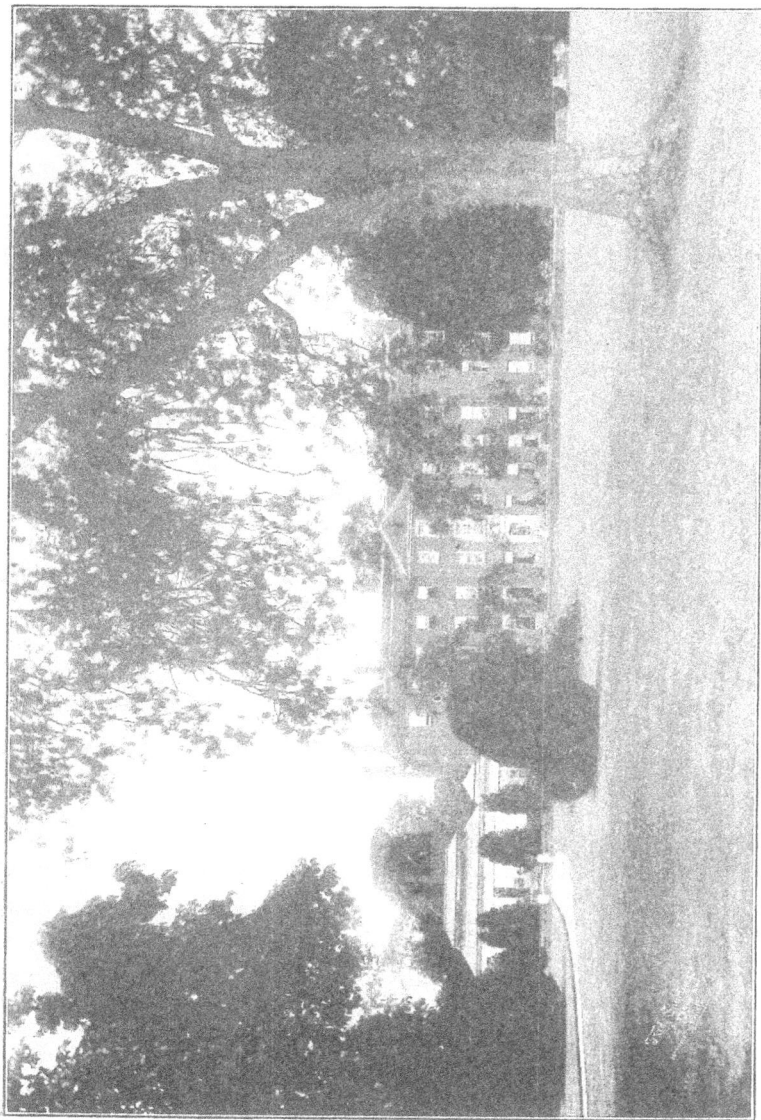

LANGLEYS, CO. ESSEX, ENGLAND.
Seat of the Everard family, rear view.

SIR RICHARD[14], 4th Baronet, was governor of North Carolina under the Lords Proprietors, and after his return to England died at his house, in Red Lion St., Holbourn, London, on 17th Febry., 1732. His widow died Sept. 12, 1739. He was succeeded by his eldest son Sir Richard[15] Everard, 5th Baronet, who died unmarried on 7th March, 1741, and was succeeded by his brother Sir Hugh Everard, 6th Baronet, who went to Georgia and married there. But dying without children in 1745, the baronetcy became extinct, and the family heritage passed to the (surviving) sister (Susanna). This is from Burke's *Extinct Baronetcies.*

To avoid confusing the similar surnames, it may be well to mention here that there was also a family of Everards, seated at Ballybay, co. Tipperary, Ireland, which included a line of baronets, whose title was created in 1622, and finally became extinct. Several of these also bore the name of Richard, but no relationship seems traceable between them and the Everards of Much Waltham, co. Essex.

The name Everard is found very much earlier than the beginning of our lineage from Burke's *Extinct and Dormant Baronetcies.* We find several mentions of it in Orderic Vitalis' *Historiae Ecclesiae.*

In Vol. II, p. 195, it is stated that Count Roger de Montgomery, one of the most prominent of the Norman nobility, and a friend of William the Conqueror, "married Adeliza, daughter of Everard du Pinset, one of the highest of the French nobility." This wife died after the birth of five sons and four daughters, and Count Roger married a second wife, "by whom he had only one son, whose name is Everard and who, being brought up to learning, became attached to the courts of William and Henry, kings of England, as one of the royal chaplains." This carries us back many years before the Norman conquest of England.

Again in Vol. II, p. 264, we find a reference to Everard, a priest of the Church of Speen, near Newbury, Berkshire. This was soon after the conquest.

Again in Vol. III, p. 78, we are told that "Everard du Poiset, among other earls and men of rank [of France], joined

Stephen, Count de Blois, son in law of William [the Conqueror], king of England, for the love of Christ in the expedition" [of the first Crusade, which followed Peter the Hermit in 1096].

Please observe that Orderic Vitalis was a contemporary, born in 1075 and died in 1143.

The following is from *Chaumiére Papers*: "My grandfather, SIR RICHARD[14] EVERARD, when a young man, was a captain in Queen Anne's army, and it is probable, was with Sir George Rooke, when he took Gibraltar, [1704], as he remained in garrison eighteen months, being so long against his inclinations, stayed there by his sense of honor altogether, he having recently married a young wife. And he resigned his commission immediately on his return to England." The young wife was Susanna Kidder.

Wright in his history of Essex says that GOVERNOR EVERARD sold the family ancestral estate to discharge debts with which it was encumbered, and afterwards purchased a smaller one at Broomfield. Having been appointed by the Lords Proprietors governor of North Carolina to succeed Governor George Burrington, he set out for America, and on 17th June, 1725, was sworn in before the Provincial Council at Edenton, as governor, captain general, admiral, and commander in chief of the colony. (*Col. Records of N. C.*, II, 556, 559).

In *North Carolina*, by Chas. L. Rapier, 1904, p. 38, we find: "George Burrington, Esqr., was the first royal governor of North Carolina. * * * He was appointed and received his commission and instructions in 1730 (Colonial Records of North Carolina, III, 65, 66, 74, 86, 87, 118, 119), but did not begin to discharge his duties until February 25, 1731 (Ibid. III, 211). SIR RICHARD[14] EVERARD, who was the last governor under the proprietors, was retained by the crown, as acting chief executive until Burrington arrived (Ibid. II, 566, 2-74, passim)". This shows conclusively that SIR RICHARD EVERARD did not leave North Carolina until after this date.

We can not go into a history of his administration in North Carolina, but refer to histories of N. C., and to a pamphlet from the publications of The Southern History Association, by

Marshall De Lancy Haywood, a copy of which we have on file.

"The only apparent event of importance which marked his administration was the settlement of the long disputed boundary question with Virginia by commissioners appointed by the two colonies for that purpose." * * *

"The younger Sir Richard, 5th baronet, was an attorney at law in North Carolina, and remained there after inheriting his father's title. He was a representative in the Provincial Assembly from Beaufort Co. in 1739, and from Bladen in 1740. (Colonial Records, IV, 346, 493). Sir Hugh, 6th baronet, succeeded his brother, and resided for some time in Georgia, where he married, but left no issue."

It is interesting to note that in the N. C. Colonial and State Records, 4, 224, in the N. C. Legislative Journal it is stated that there was "read the petition of Sir Richard[15] Everard, Bart., in behalf of Dame Susanna Everard, executrix of Sir Richard[14] Everard, decd., setting forth that the Tuskarrora Indians are indebted to the said Susanna £203 in Drest Deer Skins, and praying that they may be compelled to discharge the same. Referred to the Indian Commissioners, October 13, 1736." Dame Susanna Everard was Susanna Kidder, and Sir Richard[15] Everard was her son.

In the Library of Congress, Washington, D. C., may be found a copy of The History of the County of Essex, by Philip Morant, 1768, a large and comprehensive work and evidently a high authority. Under the title "Langleys" an interesting brief history of the Everard family is given, almost identical with that in Burke's Extinct and Dormant Baronetcies, recorded on pages 236 and f., so nearly so as to indicate that Burke has taken his account from Morant. There is some little variation, such as naturally occurs, when one person writes in his own language a description of events from the statement of another.

As stated, Morant tells us that Langleys was acquired by the Everards when THOMAS[6] EVERARD married JOAN (or Mary), daughter and heiress of JOHN CORNISH on January 7th, 1515. "The Everard family becoming thus possessed of the whole

Maner (sic) seated themselves there and many years made a considerable figure (sic)."

Morant states: "Langleys, the mansion house, stands about a quarter of a mile from the church, and is most pleasantly situated on an eminence, having the river Chelmer on the north and a brook on the south. * * * It took the name of 'Marshall' from an ancient family that flourished there from the reign of King John to that of Edward III. * * * Then it came to a family named Langley, from whom it took the name that it retains to this day. In 9 Henry IV (1421) John Langley did homage for lands he held in this parish of Walthambury."

"REV. RICHARD KIDDER, M. A., Rector of Rayne, admitted October 9th, 1664, and continued until December 23rd, 1674," is mentioned as an "eminent" rector.

He also says, that it was SIR HUGH[13] EVERARD, the father of SIR RICHARD[14], who encumbered Langleys with debt. SIR RICHARD[14] inherited it in this condition, and sold it, and bought a small estate in Broomfield parish, where his second daughter, Anne, and her husband, George Lathbury, lived for some time. Samuel Tufnell, Esqr., who bought Langleys, was very rich. He pulled down the greater part of the old house, built a good new one, made a park around it, with other improvements.

SIR RICHARD[14] EVERARD was displaced as Governor of North Carolina, when the Crown purchased it. His son, Sir Hugh, came to an empty title with a very small pittance of estate, and went to Georgia. Of the two daughters, SUSANNA[15] married in Virginia to MR. DAVID[2] MEADE, a considerable merchant there, And Anne married George Lathbury and they lived sometime at Broomfield. She must have died before the death of her brother Hugh in 1745, as the property is said then to have passed to SUSANNA.

From Coller's *The People's History of Essex*, 1861, in the writer's library, we learn much of the Everards in Essex. They lived there long before they acquired Langleys. WILLIAM[3] EVERARD, third in the lineage from Burke's *Extinct and Dormant Baronetcies*, is said to have been of Marchburg or

CHURCH OF SS. MARY AND LAWRENCE,
Great Waltham, co. Essex, England.

Marsburg, Essex, evidently the same as the parish of Mashbury, "which runs up to within five miles of Chelmsford." His
grandson, JOHN[5] EVERARD, fifth in our lineage, is said to have
been "of Newarks in Good Estre (or Easter), and Marchburg
(or Mashbury) ;" (see pages 282 and 283). These places may
be found on the map of Essex in this book, all in the neigh-
borhood of Great Waltham and Chelmsford. The next,
THOMAS[6] EVERARD, is said to have been of Great Waltham,
doubtless one of the smaller manors of that parish. He married the daughter and heiress of JOHN CORNISH, of Langleys
in Great Waltham, and at her father's death this fine estate
passed to the Everards, after 1515. This was in the reign of
Henry VIII (1509-1547). It remained in the possession of
the Everards about two hundred years, until soon after 1705,
when it was sold to Samuel Tufnell, Esqr., by SIR RICHARD[14]
EVERARD (page 250), some years before he came to America
and became Governor of North Carolina.

Great Waltham and Little Waltham constitute a parish in
Chelmsford Hundred, Essex, including the town of Chelmsford, now on the Great Eastern R. R., thirty miles N. E. of
London. Great Waltham was in 1861 divided into seven
manors, of which Langleys is the chief, with "a large and elegant mansion, surrounded by a noble park."

We also find from *The People's History of Essex* that: "The
church at Great Waltham is an ancient structure in the Norman style of the twelfth century, with some antique frescoes
upon its walls, which the hand of the modern discoverer has
brought to light from the plaster and whitewash, beneath
which they lay barbarously hidden. Part of the rood loft, and
the stoup in the porch still remain, but some of the windows
and other parts of the building are of more modern date. The
interior, which was restored and beautified about 1849, contains a number of fine and interesting monuments. * * * On
the north side, with a marble arch fourteen feet high, is a
costly monument to SIR ANTHONY[10] EVERARD, the owner of
Langleys, who was knighted in 1603, and HIS LADY. The effi-
gies are in recumbent posture with a skull and hour glass be-

hind them. An inscription in Latin tells that this splendid memorial was erected to Lady Ann Everard, daughter of Sir Thomas Barnardiston, Knt., descended from the ancient family of the Barnardistons of Kedington, in the county of Suffolk. The date of the monument is 1609, and a tablet on the left records that it was erected by her lord, who died three years after.

On the wall in the South aisle is a memorial of the deeds anl death of a scion of the same noble family, Hugh Everard, a younger son of Sir Hugh, who perished in the great storm of November 27th, 1703, in a ship, which stranded in the Goodwin Sands.

An interesting description of the neighbourhood may be found in this book.

We also get from it some interesting information of BISHOP KIDDER, whose daughter, SUSANNA, married SIR RICHARD[14] EVERARD, and was an ancestress, which will be related later.

The statement in the *Chaumiere Papers* and the impression among some of the family that Langleys, so long the family seat of the Everards, in Essex, was at one time a royal residence, is an error. This is true of a manor of this name in Cheshire, called "Langley", without the s, but not of "Langleys" in Essex. In Camden's *Brittania*, (1551), Vol. II, p. 64, we find in the description of Cheshire, "More to the South is King's Langley, formerly a royal mansion, where was born and from whence was named Edmund de Langley, son of Edward III, and Duke of York."

THE EVERARD COAT OF ARMS

In the *Chaumiére Papers* the Everard arms are described as follows:

Arms; Argent, a Fess wavy, between Estoiles, Gules;

Crest; on a wreath, a bust of a man in profile, habited in a long cap, checky;

Or Crest; on a torse, argent or gules, a man's head, couped at the shoulders, argent, and cuppe, bendy, wavy, of six, argent and sable. (See page 63.)

CHURCH OF SS. MARY AND LAWRENCE,
Great Waltham, co. Essex, England. Interior, showing Everard tombs.

About Oct. 1st, 1909, Mrs. Baskervill saw a notice in *The Southern Churchman* that Rev. Joseph L. Meade, of Alabama, (one of the Mississippi Meades), of the Episcopal Church, had gone to China as a missionary, and on the way had spent some weeks in England, and that while there "He held service in St. Mary's Church, Great Waltham, near London, which was built by one of his ancestors in 1604. He was entertained afterwards at Langley Hall nearby, where his family, the Everards, formerly lived." Finding that his address in China was "American Church Mission, Wusih, Kiang-Su, China," she wrote to him asking an account of his visit to Great Waltham. The place is also called "Waltham Magna" and "Much Waltham." He replied cordially and gave an account of a very interesting visit to Langleys, and we have his letter filed in our *"Skelton and Meade Papers,"* Vol. I. The letter was written from the above address on November 3rd, 1909.

He relates that he wrote from London to the Vicar of Great Waltham Parish, asking if he could come to see the church and the old mansion, and in reply, the Vicar and his wife called on him at his hotel in London, and not only invited him to the church and to preach there, but also delivered an invitation from the owner of Langleys to spend a week there as a guest. These invitations he accepted. He went to Chelmsford by rail, thirty miles, and thence by stage, sixteen miles, to Great Waltham. He stated that Great Waltham is a beautiful little village, and very English in every way. The deer park was very beautiful, and it is still filled with deer, but they are not hunted.

"Langleys is nothing less than a palace. It is perfectly beautiful and so well kept. Coln. and Mrs. Tufnell, who have inherited and own the place, are very well off, and spend a good deal of money on the grounds.

"SIR RICHARD[14] EVERARD sold the place (see page 84), for £300 or $1500, [money was worth about five times as much then as now—P. H. B.], and it is now worth $200,000, including the grounds. I saw the deed and letters of sale—they are at Langleys. Coln. and Mrs. Tufnell were untiring in their efforts to make my stay a pleasant one.

"The Tufnell coat of arms was placed where the Everards' once was.

"In the church everything was Everard, as the Tufnells do not bury there. The chancel was filled with graves of the family, and down each aisle are slabs and monuments of the Everards. It was quite a privilege to hold service in the church. * * *

"The drawing room at Langley extends upward through two heights of ceiling. The banquet hall is beautifully carved, and the room, which was at one time a chapel, is something marvellous.

"The Tufnells have invited me to visit them again, and I certainly intend doing so, though it is rather expensive visiting in English country homes."

Mr. Meade enclosed a photograph of himself studying Chinese with his tutor, and also two or three postal card pictures of Langleys and the vicinity. We opened correspondence with the photographer in Chelmsford, and obtained a number of photographs, small and large, of Langleys and Great Waltham, and some of the large ones have been framed and hung up in our house. Some of these will be found in our book.

Mr. Meade's health became very bad in China and he had to return to this country in February, 1911. He is now an Archdeacon in the Episcopal Church at Flagstaff, Arizona (1913).

REV. JOSEPH LYONS MEADE,
Of the Mississippi branch, studying Chinese at Wusih, China.

THE RT. REV. RICHARD KIDDER, A. M., D. D.,
Bishop of Bath and Wells, 1691-1703.
From the portrait in the Bishop's Palace.

CHAPTER VII

BISHOP RICHARD KIDDER

A. M., D. D., OF BATH AND WELLS

From Coller's *The People's History of Essex*, we learn that in 1664, twenty-seven years before he was made Bishop of Bath and Wells in 1691, Dr. KIDDER was made Rector of Rain, or Rayne Parish, in Hinckford Hundred, Essex, about six miles a little west of north from Great Waltham, as may be seen on the map in this book (*Hist. of Essex*). This close proximity accounts for the acquaintance between young RICHARD[14] EVERARD and Dr. Kidder's daughter, SUSANNA, which later developed into their marriage. Rayne Parish contains 1676 acres of land and 388 people (1861). Ravages of "the plague" occurred here in 1571, 1640 and 1665, the last after Dr. Kidder's incumbency, when "it raged for a full year, carrying off 665 persons (in this and adjacent parishes), full one-third of the population." And it is added:

> "Misery hovered o'er the doomed,
> Oft shaking from her dark and drooping wing
> The poisoned dews of death."

Some description of the conditions during the prevalence of this "plague" is given, including extracts from the *"Life of Dr. Kidder,"* evidently an autobiography written before he was a bishop. The writer's efforts to find a copy of this book in England have been unsuccessful.

The following is an abridgement of a sketch of BISHOP KIDDER by Rev. Meade C. Williams, of St. Louis, Mo., a descendant, written in January, 1899. A complete copy made by Mrs. Baskervill, is on file in our *"Skelton and Meade Papers,"* Vol. I. Mr. Williams died in 1906.

"A Vindication.

"Richard Kidder, Bishop of Bath and Wells, England, 1691-1703.

"Bishof Kidder was born in Sussex in 1633. There were nine children in the family, he being the eighth. Eight of them lived to the age of men and women, and the greater part of them to more than the sixtieth year of their age. His father had a small estate, but by reason of a kind disposition, leading him to be surety for other men, he was put to great inconvenience, so that he was able to do but little for his children.

"His mother was a very pious woman and much given to reading the Scriptures and other good books, and to prayer— so much so that the neighbors fixed upon her the name of 'Puritan.'

"He was of Emmanuel College, Cambridge. He served as parish clergyman in different places before he was appointed Bishop. In his first parish he had three children, and lost them all by death there. Afterwards other children were born, and two sons and one daughter died within three weeks.

"He had reputation as a popular preacher, and was frequently appointed as preacher or lecturer on distinguished public occasions. He also preached by invitation, twice at least, before the King and Queen, and by their order each time the sermon was printed.

"On the accession of William and Mary to the throne a number of the bishops refused to take the oath of allegiance, maintaining the claims of James II, of the House of Stuart. They became known as the 'Non-jurors'. But as the reigning house was by law the head of the church, this could not be tolerated, and these bishops were deprived of their sees. Among them was the good Bishop Ken, Bishop of Bath and Wells, although of all the clergy attached to the cathedral only four followed him in refusing the oath. But so revered was he for his personal excellence, and so did he labor under a sense of injustice in being deprived, that a strong sentiment of sympathy prevailed in his case, which seems not to have

WELLS CATHEDRAL, from St. Andrew's Spring.

been felt to the same degree in regard to the other deprived bishops. One clergyman, whom the Crown appointed as the successor of Ken at Wells (Dr. Beveridge) declined the appointment. Kidder had been offered the bishopric of Peterborough, being then the dean of that cathedral, but had refused it, and said at the time that he did not care to accept any such appointment. Subsequently he was approached again on the subject of accepting a bishopric. He then wrote his friend Dr. Williams that he would not absolutely refuse a bishop's appointment except that of Bath and Wells—that one he was not willing to accept. The ecclesiastical authorities, however, were desirous that he would take the place, and his friends reported only the first part of his answer, viz: that he would not absolutely refuse a bishopric. Archbishop Tillotson thereupon recommended him for Bath and Wells, and great persuasion and urgency were brought to bear on him to accept it, and it was the Queen's strong desire that he should do so. He was at length prevailed on to take the place, and was consecrated in the Bow Bells Church, Holborn, London, and assumed the work in 1691. He shared in the tender feeling toward Bishop Ken, his predecessor, deprived, and was much embarrassed, and felt the difficulty of the position. On first hearing of the appointment he said 'I was in such trouble and consternation as I have seldom been in during my whole life'. And he afterwards declared that he had often repented of accepting it, and looked on it as a 'great infelicity'. At the same time it must be remembered that the interests of the church required that the place should not long remain unfilled; and that other clergymen had accepted the sees of the other deprived non-jurors. The Archbishop of Canterbury and the bishops of Gloucester, Peterborough, and Ely had so done.

"Ken always cherished a bitterness towards KIDDER, with whom he had no acquaintance. He spoke of him as 'a supplanter', 'a hireling', 'a ravager of the flock', &c.

"There is nothing to show that KIDDER ever treated him with the slightest disrespect or unkindness. On the other hand he expressed tender sympathy for him. There is a tradition that he assigned or offered him part of his income as Bishop.

"KIDDER had many difficulties and troubles in his administration. He did not always have the sympathy and support of his clergy connected with the cathedral.

[This vindication is recorded here because many unjust criticisms of BISHOP KIDDER have been made in histories and other writings for accepting the bishopric of Bath and Wells].

"BISHOP KIDDER AND HIS WIFE were killed in November, 1703, by the falling of a stack of chimneys, which crushed in the roof of the room, in which they were sleeping. This was during a disastrous storm, which swept over that part of the country, and is said to have been the most violent that ever visited England. [Hugh[14] Everard, younger brother of SIR RICHARD[14] EVERARD, who married SUSANNA KIDDER, was drowned in the same storm. See page 86.] Daniel Defoe, the author of *Robinson Crusoe,* wrote a narrative of this storm and described its violence at Wells, and spoke of the BISHOP AND HIS WIFE. [In this storm also the first Eddystone lighthouse, completed in 1699, was destroyed, and the keepers, and the engineer who built it, perished with it.]

"BISHOP KIDDER was a leading divine of his day, and among the learned men of the continent of Europe he was recognized as a scholar of high merit. While he was a popular preacher, he was also an author of note, and wrote a large number of works. On the catalogue of the library of the British Museum there is an extensive list of books from his pen. He was a good Hebraist, and defended Christianity against the Jews in a three volume work. In another elaborate work he defended the Pentateuch against the free thinking critics. In this he deals with many of the points, which the 'higher critics' of the present day have brought forward as if new. An unfriendly biographer, Cassan, admits he was a very learned writer and one of the best divines of the time.

"As a churchman he evidently belonged to what in later days would be called the 'low church' wing. He was thoroughly evangelical as a theologian and as a preacher.

WELLS CATHEDRAL, Interior. Nave, showing the inverted arches.

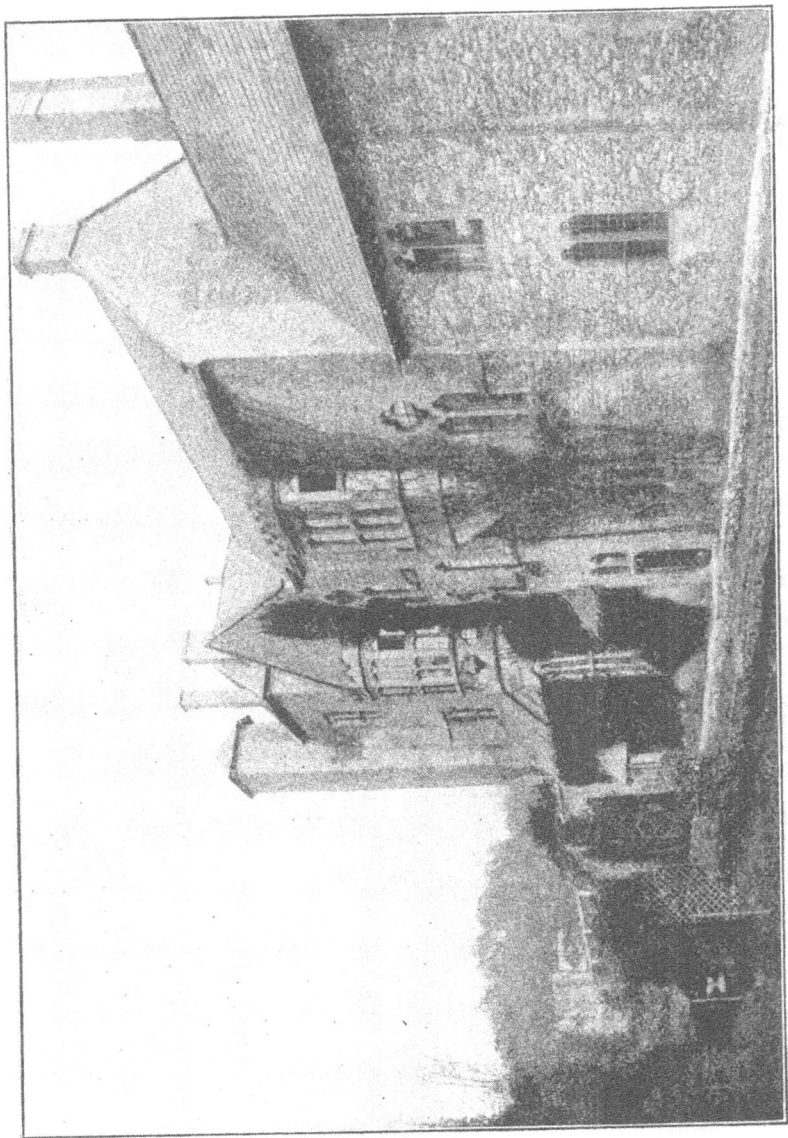

Wells Cathedral, Bishop's Palace.

"Macaulay in his *History of England* speaks of him as 'a man of considerable attainments, and blameless character, but suspected of a leaning toward Presbyterianism'.

"He was buried within the cathedral walls, and an elaborate monument was erected by his daughter [Anne] at a cost of 300 pounds. It stands in the north transept. In the epitaph [which is in Latin] is an expression of great respect for Bishop Ken.

"He left two daughters, SUSAN and Anne. Anne remained unmarried, and it was she who put up the monument. She died in 1728 (aged 38).

"SUSAN was married in the Church of St. Alphage, London, on June 13, 1706, to SIR RICHARD[14] EVERARD, BARONET, of Langleys, Essex. I saw in London a copy of the record of their marriage taken from the church register. She is there represented as being of the Parish of St. Paul's, Covent Garden, London, and he of Langleys, county of Essex.

"In as much as Priscilla Meade, sister of David[2] Meade, who married Susanna[15] Everard, married Wilson Curle, of Virginia, it may be interesting to mention that one of the predecessors of Bishop Kidder was Walter Curle, accession 1629, translated to Winchester 1632."

This ends the extracts from the statement of Rev. Meade C. Williams.

In August, 1906, the writer and his son, H. M. Baskerville, spent a day and night in Wells, and were much interested in examining the Cathedral, the bishop's palace with its portraits of the bishops, including that of BISHOP KIDDER, and the city of Wells. We brought home with us photographs of the cathedral, the palace, of Bishop Kidder, and of his tomb, copies of which were framed and hung in our home, and others sent to relatives.

The Latin inscription upon the tomb, as shown by the photograph, is very long, and a good deal defaced, and may be read with much difficulty. And there is not much that is particularly interesting or attractive about it. We have a copy of a translation of it in our *Meade Papers,* Vol. II, and will record here only the following short extract: "He had grown old in beautiful peace, a learned man, beloved alike by high and low, when on 26 November, 1703, a hurricane, which with irresistable force swept everything before it, hurled over a chimney, killing him with his faithful wife, a death which caused a sorrow relieved by the solace that without the gradual pain of dying the same blow had taken these two, who were bound together by the deepest love, venerable with years and ready to depart."

We show copies of these pictures in our book.

MURAL MONUMENT TO BISHOP KIDDER, WELLS CATHEDRAL,
North Transept.

CHAPTER VIII
THE ROYAL DESCENT

JOAN BARRINGTON

Through the marriage of SIR RICHARD[11] EVERARD to JOAN BARRINGTON (1621-1653) the family has a lineage, which traces back to many prominent and illustrious families, and to the royal family of England, and through them to the royal families of several other countries, including many illustrious princes and kings, for instance EDWARD III, WILLIAM I (the Conqueror), and ALFRED THE GREAT, of England; CHARLEMAGNE, CHARLES MARTEL, and HUGH CAPET, of France; MALCOLM III and KENNETH McALPINE of Scotland; ROLLO, THE DANE, who established the Duchy of Normandy, and many others. The tracing back to about 500 A. D. seems to be absolutely authoritative, and genealogists have carried the line of Alfred the Great back to 90 B. C., and others, including the *"Anglo-Saxon Chronicle"*, back to Adam. We refer to the table on page 74, which is interesting and remarkable. But we come back to JOAN BARRINGTON.

THE BARRINGTONS were an old family, which date back to the time of WILLIAM, THE CONQUEROR, when BARENTONE, A SAXON, had the custody of the forest of Hatfield Regis. From him through his son, EUSTACHIUS DE BARENTONE and twelve other generations the lineage is traced to

JOHN BARRINGTON, ESQR., living in 1534, whose seat and estate was in Essex. He was succeeded by his son THOMAS BARRINGTON, ESQR., who married secondly WINIFRED POLE, daughter of HENRY POLE, LORD MONTAGUE, whose son was

SIR FRANCIS BARRINGTON, KNT., M. P. for Essex, married JOAN CROMWELL, aunt of Oliver Cromwell, whose daughter JOAN BARRINGTON (above) married SIR RICHARD[11] EVERARD.

From Brown's *Genesis of America*, p. 825, we get: "Sir Francis Barrington, great grandson of George, Duke of Clarence, brother to Edward IV, was M. P. for Essex in 1601; knighted at Theobald's May 7th, 1603; M. P. for Essex 1621-22, 1624, 1626, 1627 and 1628; died July 3rd, 1628. He married Joan, daughter of Sir Henry Cromwell, and aunt of the Protector, Cromwell. Their daughter Joan married Sir Richard Everard, and Bishop Wm. Meade, of Virginia, was a descendant of theirs. Lady Joan Barrington survived her husband. See the letters written to her by Rev. Roger Williams in 1629, published in the *New England Register*, July 1889, pp. 316-320."

The Cromwell Family

This family was not ancient or conspicuous, except for two of its members, Thomas, Lord Cromwell, very conspicuous during the reign of Henry VIII, but not to be admired, and Oliver Cromwell, the "Protector", too well known to need comment. We refer to our Cromwell Table on page 68, and to history.

Notes from Pepy's Diary, Vol. I, page 27: "Sir Henry Cromwell, son [grandson] of Richard Williams, who had assumed the name of Cromwell, and whose grandson, Sir Oliver, was the uncle and godfather of the Protector.

"Col. Williams (Cromwell that was) appears to have been Henry Cromwell, grandson of Sir Oliver Cromwell and first cousin, once removed, to the Protector. He changed his name, knowing that Cromwell would not be popular to the Court, he disused it, and assumed that of Williams, which had belonged to his ancestors. He died in 1673."

A reference to our Cromwell table will explain this.

The Pole Family

THOMAS BARRINGTON, ESQR., married WINIFRED POLE, as stated. The most conspicuous member of this family was

Cardinal Reginald Pole, who was very prominent in the Roman Catholic Church, and during the reign of Queen Mary, daughter and successor of Henry VIII, attempted to restore Roman Catholicism in England, and went out of favor when she died in 1558. He was a younger brother of Henry Pole, Lord Montague, who was father of our ancestress, Winifred Pole.

The first of the family of whom anything memorable occurred was

SIR RICHARD POLE, KNT., son of SIR JEFFREY POLE, KNT., of an ancient Welsh family, the former being a commander of the troops of Henry VII in his wars with Scotland, and also a Knight of the Garter. He married LADY MARGARET PLANTAGANET, Countess of Salisbury, daughter of GEORGE, DUKE OF CLARENCE, who (she) was executed when seventy years old, the "Last of the Plantaganets." The Pole family was quite conspicuous and historical.

THE MORTIMER FAMILY

ANNE MORTIMER married RICHARD PLANTAGANET, EARL OF CAMBRIDGE, and they were the grandparents of Edward IV, GEORGE, DUKE OF CLARENCE, and Richard III. See the table on page 67.

This family trace back to ROGER DE MORTIMER, a prominent nobleman of Normandy, whose record precedes the Battle of Hastings. He was by consanguinity allied to William, the Conqueror, his MOTHER being neice to Gunnora, wife of Richard I, Duke of Normandy, and great grandfather to the Conqueror. There is a record of ROGER, that in 1054 he lived in his baronial Castle de Caux, in Pays de Caux, Normandy. In this year WILLIAM sent him in command of an army to repel an invasion, in which he was successful. On the invasion of England he contributed sixty vessels to the Duke's fleet. His son was RALPH DE MORTIMER, and it seems that both ROGER and RALPH participated in the Battle of Hastings. In *Domesday Book*, about 1083, RALPH is said to have possessed one hundred and twenty-three manors, besides several hamlets, and the castle of Wigmore, which became the seat of the family.

After these the line continued through ten generations, conspicuous and powerful, particularly as Earls of March, to ROGER MORTIMER slain in battle in Ireland, whose daughter ANNE[13] MORTIMER married RICHARD PLANTAGENET, EARL OF CAMBRIDGE, in the table.

For details see *The Conqueror and His Companions*, Planché, in our library, and Burke's *Extinct Peerages and Baronetcies* in the Va. State Library.

THE PLANTAGENETS

MARGARET PLANTAGENET, Countess of Salisbury, wife of SIR RICHARD POLE, Knt., was a near descendant of the royal family of England of that name, and died, or rather was executed, the last of them.

THE PLANTAGENETS were a turbulent race, their private history is not pleasing, and generally these were troublous times in England. Among the nobility each man seemed to try to supplant his neighbor, or probably his brother or kinsman, and murder was lightly thought of. Those in power seemed disposed to kill brothers and cousins and neighbors to prevent opposition in their ambition. And many members of the Plantagenet family were murdered, executed, or slain in battle. This was the time of the "Wars of the Roses", and English history consists chiefly of wars and murders among relatives. And the record is not attractive.

THE PLANTAGENETS came from France. GEOFFREY PLANTAGENET, COUNT OF ANJOU, married MATILDA, daughter of HENRY I, KING OF ENGLAND, and their son became HENRY II. From him in direct male descent through five generations came EDWARD III, one of the greatest of the English kings, and after him came the Wars of the Roses between the descendants of two of his sons. ANNE MORTIMER and her husband, RICHARD, EARL OF CAMBRIDGE, were both descended from him through different sons, the one in the fourth generation and the other in the third. And MARGARET PLANTAGENET,

COUNTESS OF SALISBURY, was their great granddaughter. See the tables for the details.

These notes might be continued almost indefinitely, but it is probably not desirable. Any student of history may follow up numerous other lines for himself.

HARDAWAY FAMILY

THE HARDAWAY FAMILY.

Thomas[1] Hardaway, came from England about 1685; settled at "Osborns", Chesterfield Co.; d. 1745. m. Jane { Stith, dau. of Drewry Stith (Southall). Drewry (Hubert). See text.

John[2] Hardaway, b. 1708, m. Frances Markham.

Daniel[2] or Stith[2] } Hardaway, m. 1st, Martha Worsham, 2nd, Purify Booker, no issue.

Thomas[2] Hardaway, b. 1715, m. Agnes Peterson.

James[2] Hardaway, b. 1719, d. 1770, m. Millian Stanfield in 1756.

William[2] Hardaway, b. 1723, m. —— Manson.

Frances[2] Hardaway, b. 1725, m. William Skipwith; both died in London.

Joseph[2] Hardaway, b. 1728, m. Anna Hall.

Drewry[2] Hardaway, b. 1733, probably died infant.

Daniel[3] Hardaway, m. Anne Eggleston. See Eggleston Family.

Stith[3] Hardaway, d. unm.

Judith[3] Archer H. m. —— Lewis.

Dr. Daniel[4] Hardaway, m. Sally Jones.

Martha[4] Hardaway, m. 1, Edwin Harvie, 2, Wm. Old.

John[4] Segar Hardaway, m. Martha Fletcher.

Maria[4] Hardaway, m. Seth W. Jones; went to Mississippi. 3 children living now.

Richard[4] Eggleston H., m. Mary Rutherfoord.

Jane[4] Elizabeth H., m. Benj. L. Meade. See Meade Family.

Stith[4] Lewis.

Caroline[4] Lewis.

Martha[4] Lewis.

Judith[4] Lewis.

a   b   c   d   e

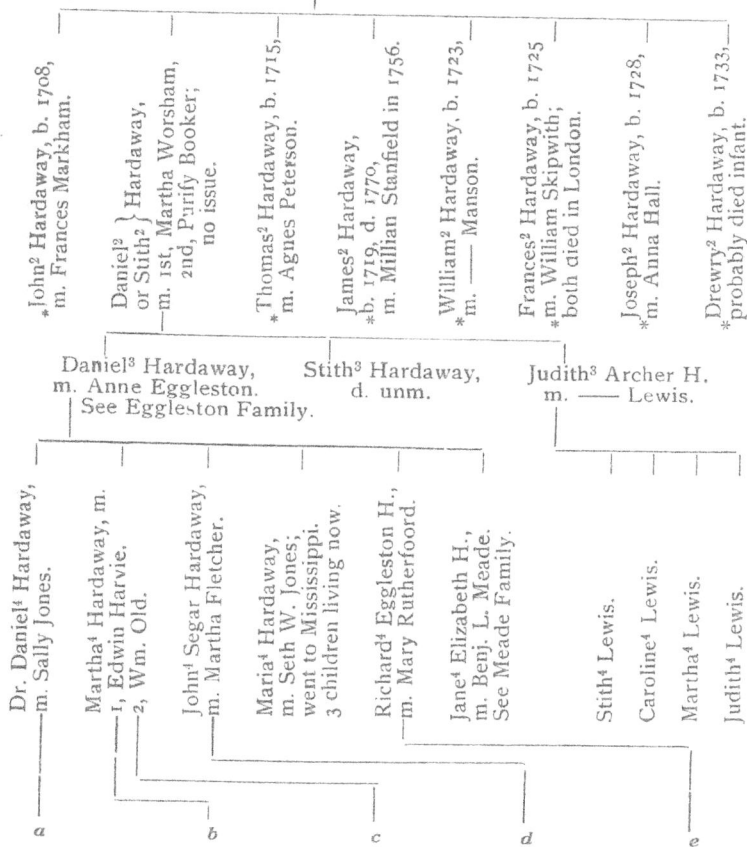

*These lines are fully given in Mrs. Hubert's *Thomas Hardaway and His Descendants*, in our library. They are too long to be included here.

John Hardaway is said by Mr. Southall probably to have been a brother of Thomas[1] Hardaway (and not son), but Mrs. Hubert's statement, that he was a son, seems to be most probably correct.

a

Horace[5] Hardaway,
—m. Sally Anne Hardaway.

Anne[5] Hardaway,
m. Wm. Fitzgerald.

Daniel[6] Hardaway.

John[6] Hardaway.

Richard[6] Hardaway.

Margaret[6] Hardaway.

Harvie[6] Hardaway.

Sally[6] Hardaway.

b

Lewis[5] Harvie,
m. Sarah Blair.

Dr. John[5] Harvie,
—m. Mary Blair.

Sarah[6] B. Harvie,
m. R. B. Chaffin.

Dr. Lewis[6] E. Harvie,
m. Martha Rutherfoord.

James[6] B. Harvie,
m. Lou. Michaux.

Mary[6] W. Harvie,
m. N. R. Ruffin.

Eliza[6] M. Harvie, unm.

Martha[6] O. Harvie, unm.

c

William[5] Old,
m. Judith Eggleston.

Charles[5] Old,
m. Anne Carter Leigh.

d

Jacqueline[5] Hardaway,
m. Freeman Epes.

Sally[5] Anne Hardaway,
m. Horace Hardaway.

Blair[6] Harvie,
m. John L. Waring.

Fannie[6] Harvie,
m. Peachy Dance.

e

John[5] Segar Hardaway,
m. Sally Steger.
6 sons and 5 daughters.

HARDAWAY FAMILY—Continued.

The following chart is made from an article in the William and Mary Quarterly, Vol. XX, p. 216 (Jany., 1912), and the variations are marked *. See page 109.

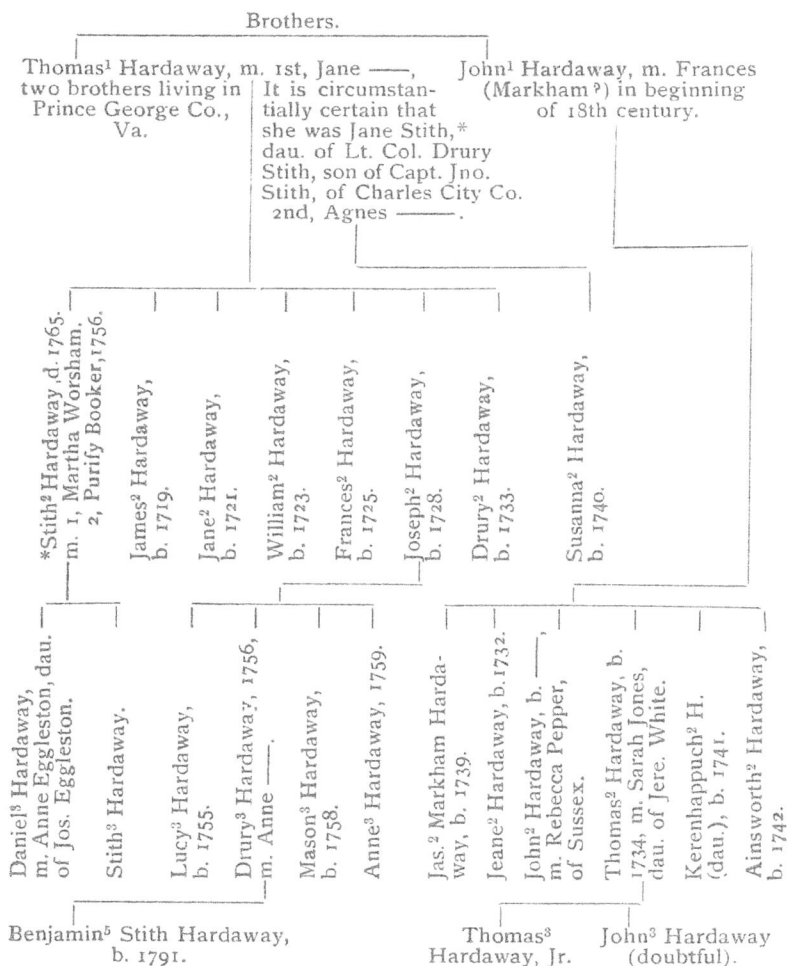

Brothers.

Thomas¹ Hardaway, m. 1st, Jane ——, two brothers living in Prince George Co., Va. | It is circumstantially certain that she was Jane Stith,* dau. of Lt. Col. Drury Stith, son of Capt. Jno. Stith, of Charles City Co. 2nd, Agnes ——. | John¹ Hardaway, m. Frances (Markham?) in beginning of 18th century.

*Stith² Hardaway, d. 1765. m. 1, Martha Worsham. 2, Purify Booker, 1756.

James² Hardaway, b. 1719.

Jane² Hardaway, b. 1721.

William² Hardaway, b. 1723.

Frances² Hardaway, b. 1725.

Joseph² Hardaway, b. 1728.

Drury² Hardaway, b. 1733.

Susanna² Hardaway, b. 1740.

Daniel³ Hardaway, m. Anne Eggleston, dau. of Jos. Eggleston.

Stith³ Hardaway.

Lucy³ Hardaway, b. 1755.

Drury³ Hardaway, 1756, m. Anne ——.

Mason³ Hardaway, b. 1758.

Anne³ Hardaway, 1759.

Jas.² Markham Hardaway, b. 1739.

Jeane² Hardaway, b.1732.

John² Hardaway, b. —— m. Rebecca Pepper, of Sussex.

Thomas² Hardaway, b. 1734, m. Sarah Jones, dau. of Jere. White.

Kerenhappuch² H. (dau.), b. 1741.

Ainsworth² Hardaway, b. 1742.

Benjamin⁵ Stith Hardaway, b. 1791.

Thomas³ Hardaway, Jr.

John³ Hardaway (doubtful).

CHAPTER IX

THE HARDAWAY FAMILY

JANE ELIZABETH HARDAWAY, b. 1801, d. 1876, on July 10th, 1819, married BENJAMIN L. MEADE, and these were Mrs. Baskervill's grandparents.

We do not attempt to write a comprehensive history of this family, nor to present a full roll of the later generations, but only to include the earlier history in Virginia, and then the branch of the family with which the Meades are connected.

Our information in regard to the family is derived from several sources. Several years ago we found accidentally in a book shop in Albany, N. Y., a small family history, called *Thomas Hardaway and His Descendants,* by Mrs. Sarah Donelson Hubert, of Norwood, Warren Co., Georgia, 1906, a descendant, well written, but with probably some inaccuracies, as all such books have. From this we get the most of our history.

The family has from the beginning increased rapidly, and is much scattered through the Southern States, and our branch, descended from one of the sons of the first THOMAS HARDAWAY, seem to have had little or no knowledge of the other branches. Very little space is given to our branch in Mrs. Hubert's book, and that of John[2] Hardaway, her ancestor, occupies about two-thirds of her book, as is natural.

Another source of information is an article in the *William and Mary Quarterly,* of January, 1912, page 216, written by Rev. S. O. Southall, of Amelia Co., together with a letter, which he kindly sent to the writer in answer to an inquiry on Febry. 25, 1914. This information differs in some important points in the early history from Mrs. Hubert's book, and Mr. Southall's statements seem to be authoritative and correct. These will be treated later.

A third source of information is a statement sent many years ago to Mrs. Baskervill by the late Mrs. James Eggleston, of Richmond, Va., but written by some one else. This has a good deal of information in it, but is stated to have been written from memory, and is so full of errors as to be unreliable.

From Mrs. Hubert's book we get the earliest history in Virginia.

THOMAS[1] HARDAWAY, the emigrant, said to be the ancestor of all the Hardaways in America, came from England when a small boy about 1685. He is said to have been kidnapped and brought over in a ship owned by Joseph Thomas, a Quaker, of Philadelphia. "Tradition says that he was kidnapped and held for a ransom, but his captors, perhaps getting in a close place, had put him in the hold of the outgoing ship to get rid of him." Joseph Thomas named him Thomas Hardaway and educated him. He is said, when found, to have been "dressed in green silk velvet trimmed with gilt, seemed tenderly nurtured, and was too young to give his name."

"He married JANE DREWRY, of Drewry's Bluff, Va., and settled at Osborn's, Chesterfield Co., Va. Their children intermarried with colonial families of respect, wealth, and arms bearing people. From THOMAS HARDAWAY AND JANE DREWRY I suppose all the Hardaways in America are descended."

"From the *Bristol Parish Register* [Va.] we find: 'In 1733 the vestry of Bristol Parish met May 4th at the house of MR. THOMAS HARDAWAY, near the chapel at the Ferry, and agreed to build the brick church at Wells Hill, now known as Blandford Church in Petersburg. For more than twenty years THOMAS HARDAWAY was a member of Blandford Church, though known then as Brick Church, and previously as Ferry Chapel, then located in Chesterfield Co.'

"From the Virginia Land Registry office, Richmond, Va., we find that THOMAS HARDAWAY patented the following tracts of land:

"May 2, 1713, 288 acres in Charles City Co.;

"Sept. 28th, 1728, 300 acres in Brunswick Co.;

"Sept. 28, 1730, 400 acres and 354 acres in Prince George Co.; [from which Dinwiddie Co. was later taken]."

Mrs. Eggleston's statement relates that the emigration occurred "about 1619 to 1632," but a reference to the other dates of THOMAS HARDAWAY shows that this is inaccurate, and we accept Mrs. Hubert's date of "about 1685."

We continue Mrs. Hubert's statement:

"THOMAS HARDAWAY AND JANE DREWRY, his wife, had seven sons and one daughter, viz.:

I. John² Hardaway, born 1708, married Frances Markham about 1728;

II. DANIEL² HARDAWAY, b. 1711, m. MARTHA WORSHAM;

III. Thomas² Hardaway, b. 1715, m. Agnes Peterson;

IV. James² Hardaway, b. July 10, 1719, m. Millian Stanfield 1756, d. 1770;

V. William² Hardaway, b. June 12, 1723, m. —— Manson;

VI. Frances² Hardaway, b. Apl. 4, 1725, m. Wm. Skipwith, eldest son and heir of Sir Wm. Skipwith, Baronet;

VII. Joseph² Hardaway, b. Mch. 1728, m. Ann Hall;

VIII. Drewry² Hardaway, b. Apl. 2, 1733, supposed to have died in infancy."

Of these DANIEL² HARDAWAY, or rather STITH² HARDAWAY, which we shall find was most probably his correct name, and his wife, Martha Worsham, were ancestors of our branch of the family. Frances, VI, and her husband, Wm. Skipwith, had no children. They both died early, and Sir. Wm. Skipwith, the father, was succeeded by his second son, Peyton; and Drewry Hardaway, VII, is supposed to have died in infancy. The other sons had families and many children, and their very numerous descendants are widely scattered in Virginia and the other Southern States, as previously stated. The largest number of them seem to have gone to Georgia, where they are numerous and scattered, the next largest number to Alabama, and there are others in South Carolina, Tennessee, and Mississippi, and some in California. Those in Virginia seem to have been in the counties of Dinwiddie, Nottoway, Lunenburg, Brunswick and Charles City.

Mrs. Hubert apparently gives an exhaustive register of these with some history. The number of descendants by name in her book far exceeds five hundred and it is not practicable for us to include them in this sketch, either in our table or in our text, and we shall have to confine ourselves to DANIEL² (or STITH²) HARDAWAY and his descendants, including our branch. We will mention, however, that John³ Hardaway, of Nottoway Co., Va., son of Thomas² Hardaway, already mentioned, of Hardaway Mills, Nottoway Co., Va., was a major in the Continental Army; and that Benjamin⁴ Hardaway, son of Thomas³, son of Thomas², was a captain in the United States Army in 1812. All of this information comes from Mrs. Hubert's book.

And now taking up Rev. Mr. Southall's papers we find several variations of importance from Mrs. Hubert's statements. And first, where Mrs. Hubert states that the first John Hardaway was the oldest son of THOMAS¹ HARDAWAY, Mr. Southall states: "About the beginning of the 18th century two Hardaways—THOMAS and John—were living in Prince George Co., Va. They were probably brothers.

"I. THOMAS¹ HARDAWAY married Jane ————. It is circumstantially certain that she was JANE STITH, daughter of LT. COL. DRURY STITH, son of CAPT. JOHN STITH, of Charles City Co. They had issue:

1. STITH² (the proof is circumstantial);
2. James, b. 7-10-1719 (*Bristol Parish Register*);
3. Jane, b. 3-26-1721;
4. William, b. 6-12-1723;
5. Frances, b. 4-4-1725;
6. Joseph, b. 3-9-1728;
7. Drury, b. 4-2-1733." Please notice that the lineage is carried back through JANE STITH and her father DRURY STITH to CAPT. JOHN STITH, which probably opens a line of interesting investigation in this direction.

Here we have several variations from Mrs. Hubert's list. First as to John Hardaway, who, she says, was the oldest son of THOMAS¹ HARDAWAY, but according to Mr. Southall he was "probably" his brother. Now if we take Mrs. Hubert's traditional story of THOMAS HARDAWAY as true, it seems impossible for them to have been brothers, and as Mr. Southall's account is only a probability, it seems, more reasonable to accept Mrs. Hubert's account. We do not know whether Mr. Southall had any knowledge of Mrs. Hubert's book or the traditional story—we suppose not.

Secondly, Mr. Southall states: "It is circumstantially certain that THOMAS[1] HARDAWAY married JANE STITH, daughter of LT. COLN. DRURY STITH, son of CAPT. JOHN STITH," [and not "Jane Drewry, of Drewry's Bluff"]. This seems very probably correct, especially in consideration of what will follow here. Please observe that COLN. STITH's first name was Drury, and that may have led to the impression in Mrs. Hubert's statement.

Thirdly, the second son of THOMAS[1] in Mrs. Hubert's list, there named "DANIEL"[2], the ancestor of our branch of the family, is named by Mr. Southall "STITH"[2], and Mr. Southall seems certainly to be correct. He goes on to state: "STITH[2] HARDAWAY (THOMAS[1]) married twice: I. MARTHA WORSHAM. There is a record in Chesterfield Co., which states that JOHN WORSHAM, of Henrico, gave a certain tract of land to his son DANIEL, who died, and the land descended to his three daughters—Phoebe, wife of John Booker; Elizabeth, wife of John Royall, and MARTHA, WIFE OF STITH HARDAWAY. The same records assert that she was then dead leaving two sons, Daniel[3] and Stith[3]. Stith[2] Hardaway married in 1756, 2nd Purify Booker, by whom he had no issue. He died in Amelia Co. in 1765 and in his will names his son, Stith[3]. Another record in *Virginia Magazine*, IX, 214, shows that DANIEL WORSHAM married JUDITH ARCHER, who married 2dly Col. Edward Booker, of Winterham, Amelia Co., who died in 1750. She was a daughter of JOHN ARCHER, of Bermuda Hundred, who died in 1718."

These statements are based upon the Chesterfield Co. records and seem to be authoritative. We have an abstract of the will of Stith[2] Hardaway referred to. Mr. Southall wrote us that he knew of a pedigree left by Mr. John Hardaway, in which it is stated: "My great grandfather, DANIEL HARDAWAY married MISS WORSHAM," and added: "Of course this is wrong; his great grandfather was STITH, not Daniel, and it was Stith, who married Miss Worsham. STITH[2] may have had other children besides DANIEL[3] and Stith[3], but there is no mention of them in the records."

Mr. Southall is an experienced and intelligent genealogist and so we seem compelled to accept his authoritative statements that THOMAS HARDAWAY married JANE STITH, and that our ancestor in the second generation was named STITH and not Daniel.

Also Mrs. Hubert mentions a daughter of (DANIEL) STITH[2] HARDAWAY, named Judith[3] Archer Hardaway, who married ———— Lewis, and who is not mentioned by Mr. Southall. STITH[2] HARDAWAY in his will mentioned only one son, Stith[3], but the will was "witnessed by DANIEL[3] HARDAWAY, son and heir at law of the said STITH[2] HARDAWAY." But no mention was made of a daughter.

We have also another source of information, *The Bristol Parish Vestry Book and Register,* copies of which may be found in the library of the Virginia Historical Society, and in the Virginia State Library. There are seventeen references to THOMAS[1] HARDAWAY, from 1727 to 1743, chiefly records of land processioning done by him, and also the baptisms of five of his children, giving the dates. His wife is called "Jane Hardaway," and there is nothing to show whether she was Jane Drewry or Jane Stith. The other Hardaway references are records of baptisms of later members of the family with the dates, which is useful, and also establishes the fact that John[2] Hardaway married Frances Markham, which otherwise was somewhat doubtful. In these are included children of John[2], Thomas[2], and Joseph[2], but none of our branch, and nothing to show whether our ancestor was named Daniel or Stith. The tradition that he was named Daniel certainly existed in Virginia as well as Georgia, as Mrs. Eggleston's statement shows, and also "the pedigree left by Mr. John Hardaway," referred to by Mr. Southall.

THOMAS[1] HARDAWAY is mentioned in the *Bristol Parish Vestry Book and Register* as late as 1743, and he is said to have died in 1745, which seems to confirm the accuracy of his emigration 'about 1685."

This book does not go back of 1719 and therefore the baptisms of John[2] and STITH (OR DANIEL[2]) are not recorded there.

Referring back to the Worshams on page 111, they were a family of Huguenots, who settled at Manakin, Va., of good standing and well connected. It looks as if JOHN WORSHAM, father of DANIEL, and grandfather of MARTHA WORSHAM HARDAWAY, was a son of WILLIAM AND ELIZABETH WORSHAM, parents of Elizabeth Worsham, who married Richard Kennon. The dates correspond and at this early period this William Worsham and his brother George, who jointly patented lands in 1652, and their families, were probably the only persons of this name in the country. See Worsham family in *Baskerville Genealogy* (in the Va. State Library).

Of the third generation in our branch of the Hardaway family, Stith[3] Hardaway died unmarried; please remember that Mrs. Hubert says that there was a daughter Judith[3] Archer Hardaway, who married ———— Lewis, not mentioned by Mr. Southall, and the descendants of Daniel[3] Hardaway, the oldest son, and his wife Anne Eggleston will be found in our table, through the fifth generation, but we can not attempt to give any history of them. That can be done better by members of the family on the blank pages in the back of this book, as the writer has little information in regard to them. The descendants of the other members of the second generation may be found in Mrs. Hubert's book.

EGGLESTON FAMILY

EGGLESTON FAMILY.

*Richard[1] Eggleston, came over in 1635.

*Richard[2] Eggleston, in Indian fight of 1656.

Joseph[3] Eggleston, m. †Anne Pettus,　　　Possibly Benj.[3] Eggleston.
　　d. 1730.　　　　b. 1702, d. 1736.

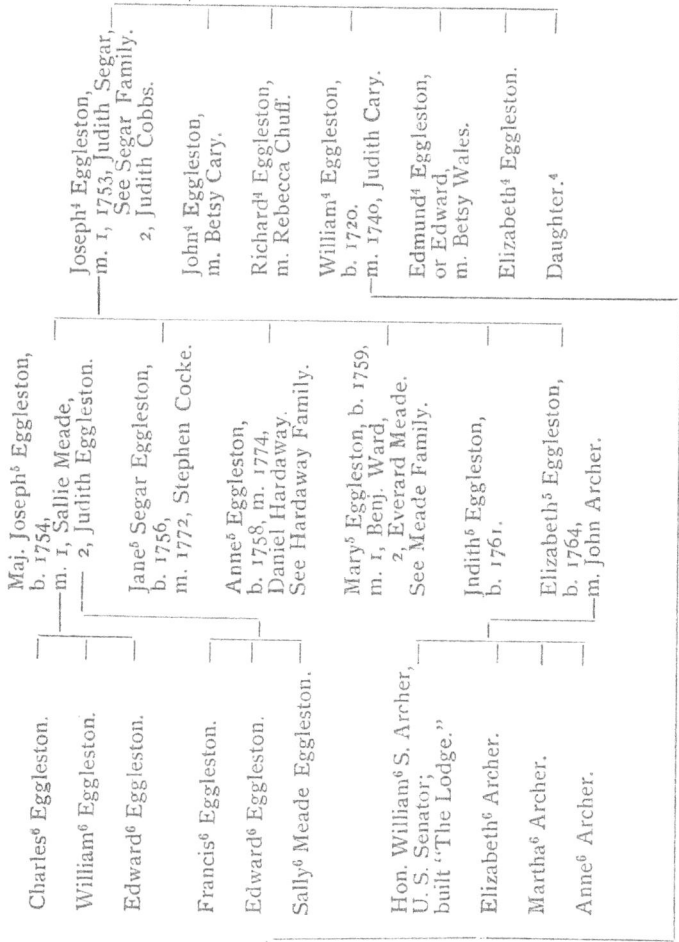

Joseph[4] Eggleston, m. 1, 1753, Judith Segar, See Segar Family. 2, Judith Cobbs.

John[4] Eggleston, m. Betsy Cary.

Richard[4] Eggleston, m. Rebecca Chuff.

William[4] Eggleston, b. 1720. m. 1740, Judith Cary.

Edmund[4] Eggleston, or Edward, m. Betsy Wales.

Elizabeth[4] Eggleston.

Daughter.[4]

Maj. Joseph[5] Eggleston, b. 1754, m. 1, Sallie Meade, 2, Julith Eggleston.

Jane[5] Segar Eggleston, b. 1756, m. 1772, Stephen Cocke.

Anne[5] Eggleston, b. 1758, m. 1774, Daniel Hardaway. See Hardaway Family.

Mary[5] Eggleston, b. 1759, m. 1, Benj. Ward, 2, Everard Meade. See Meade Family.

Judith[5] Eggleston, b. 1761.

Elizabeth[5] Eggleston, b. 1764, m. John Archer.

Charles[6] Eggleston.

William[6] Eggleston.

Edward[6] Eggleston.

Francis[6] Eggleston.

Edward[6] Eggleston.

Sally[6] Meade Eggleston.

Hon. William[6] S. Archer, U. S. Senator; built "The Lodge."

Elizabeth[6] Archer.

Martha[6] Archer.

Anne[6] Archer.

a

a

Edward[5] Eggleston.   Matthew[5] Eggleston.   Richard[5] Eggleston.   Wm.[5] Cary Eggleston.   Joseph[5] Eggleston.   Judith[5] Cary Eggleston, m. Maj. Jos. Eggleston.   Anne[5] Eggleston.

See Goode's *Virginia Cousins*, 279.

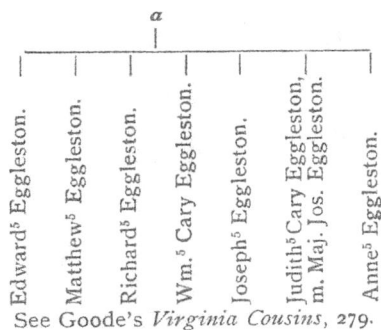

*The first two generations are said to be conjectural.
†Anne Pettus is said to have been Jos.[3] Eggleston's second wife.

CHAPTER X

THE EGGLESTON FAMILY

MARY[5] EGGLESTON, daughter of JOSEPH[4] EGGLESTON, married first Benjamin Ward, and after his death GENL. EVERARD[3] MEADE.

Our information in regard to the Eggleston family comes from quite a number of sources, but the amount is rather small.

There are families of this name in Virginia and Connecticut, but if there is a connection, it has not been traced. The Connecticut family spell the name with one g, but considering the great variation in the spelling of proper names this is not necessarily of any significance.

In a newspaper article in the *Times-Dispatch* about 1895, of which we have a copy, it is stated that the Connecticut family is "descended from Bagot Egleston, born in England, who married Mary Talcott, and in 1674 settled at Windsor, Conn., where he died." Their coat of arms is described: "Argent; a cross sable, 1st quarter a fleur de lis; Crest; a Talbot's head erased sable, collared argent. Motto: In Cruce Salus." It is said that the Virginia family, although no connection is traced, claim them as the same stock and use the coat of arms.

There are conflicting statements as to the origin of the Virginia Egglestons.

From Hotten's *The Original Lists of Persons of Quality,* &c., 1600-1700, we learn that two persons named Richard Eggleston came to Virginia from England in the ship *"Transport"*, Edward Walker, master, sailing from London July 4th, 1635, "upon certificate from the minister of Gravesend of his conformitie to the orders and discipline of the Church of England", one twenty-four years old, and the other sixteen.

And one of these is said to have been the first of the family in Virginia.

From Goode's *Virginia Cousins* we get: "The Egglestons, long seated in Virginia, are believed to have been of Irish origin. The first of the name in the colony was RICHARD[1] EGGLESTON, who came over in 1635 and settled on the "Eastern Shore" of Virginia.

RICHARD[2] EGGLESTON, who in 1656 participated in the disastrous fight against the Indians at the Falls of the James, was perhaps his son, while

JOSEPH[3] EGGLESTON, of Powhatan or Amelia Co., was perhaps grandson of the first and son of the second. These probably constitute the first three generations."

It must be admitted that this seems to be somewhat conjectural.

The newspaper article mentioned states: "Joseph Eggleston emigrated from Wales or Ireland and settled near Hampton, Va. He was father of Joseph Eggleston, who lived at 'Powhatan', above Williamsburg" [James City Co.].

From Bishop Meade's *Old Families of Virginia* we get: "The following is from an ancient lady: The Egglestons are of Irish extract, but came over to this country from England, and settled first on the Eastern Shore of Virginia. After some time two brothers, William and Joseph, came to Amelia Co., and located near the central position, where they lived to the time of their death." (This will be continued later.)

Again in a letter of Mrs. Judith Eggleston Old (Mrs. Wm. Old) it was stated: "Eggleston is a Welsh name and signifies 'the keystone of an arch'. JOSEPH[3] EGGLESTON, SR., emigrated from England and settled near Hampton, Va. His wife was ANN PETTIS [or Pettus] of Hanover Co.; issue five sons and two daughters. JOSEPH[4] and William[4] settled in Amelia Co., Va. JOSEPH[4] EGGLESTON, who became the father of Major Joseph Eggleston, had no war record, [was] simply a fine old country gentleman. His [Joseph, Jr's.] wife was JUDITH SEGAR of Middlesex Co., Va."

Here we have several conflicting traditional statements, and are told that the matter of the earlier generations can not be definitely solved on account of the loss of the James City county records, and in our table we have adopted what seems to be the most probable solution.

The Virginia land books show that Richard Eggleston on March 9th, 1653, patented 900 acres of land; on May 25th, 1655, 62½ acres, and on March 18th, 1662, 1377 A. 58 chs., all in James City Co. This was doubtless the emigrant, and he may have settled elsewhere earlier and now removed to James City Co.

Also from the same we find that Benjamin Eggleston patented 595 acres on Oct. 23rd, 1690, and 1670 acres on April 26th, 1698, in James City Co. This was doubtless a son of Richard, who received the earlier grants, or he may have belonged to the third generation.

The Journal of the House of Burgesses in the Virginia Historical Society library shows that JOSEPH³ EGGLESTON represented James City Co. in that body from 1727 until his death (1730). His last attendance was on July 3rd, 1730, and on May 19th, 1732, a writ was issued ordering an election for his successor, he being dead. The dates show that this must have been JOSEPH³ of our table, and also that it was not JOSEPH³, but JOSEPH⁴, who went to Amelia. Bishop Meade (II, 20) says: "The following is from high authority: Joseph Eggleston, Sen., moved to Amelia Co. in 1758 or 59, as shown by the baptism of his third child by the Rev. John Fox, in Ware parish, Gloucester Co., [just across York river from James City Co.], in 1758; and of his fourth child by the Rev. John Brunskell, in Raleigh parish, Amelia Co., in 1759, as recorded in his Bible, now in the possession of his family." It is true that on the death of JOSEPH³, JOSEPH⁴ *became* Joseph, Senior, and his son Joseph, Junior. But this is apt to mislead, because JOSEPH³, the first Joseph, is usually considered JOSEPH, SR.

And now we give another source of information, very authoritative, because it was evidently written by JOSEPH⁴ EGGLESTON.

A very interesting statement in regard to the Egglestons was found in a *Bible History*, of 1703, at "Egglestetton",

Amelia Co., Va., the seat of the family, evidently written by
JOSEPH⁴ EGGLESTON, father of Major Joseph⁵ Eggleston, is as
follows:

"Jane⁵ Segar Eggleston was married to Stephen Cocke, of
Amelia Co., on March 5th, 1772.

"Anne⁵ Eggleston was married to Daniel Hardaway (grandson of Thomas Hardaway, who came from England in 1685),
of Amelia Co., Sept. 5th, 1774."

"MARY⁵ EGGLESTON was married to Benjamin Ward, of
Chesterfield Co., Jany. 23rd, 1779, and their first child, Seth
Ward, born Jany. 7th, 1780.

"Benjamin Ward, husband to my daughter Mary, departed
this life (after a lingering illness of nearly eighteen months)
the 30th April, in the year of our Lord 1783.

"Joseph⁵ Eggleston married Sallie Meade, daughter of
Everard Meade, March 8th, 1788.

"Elizabeth⁵ Eggleston married John Archer, of Amelia Co.,
May 24th, 1788."

And another interesting statement was copied from mem-
oranda written on the fly leaves of an old Prayer Book, edition
of 1758, at Egglestetton, supposed to have been made by
Major Joseph⁵ Eggleston, or his father:

"JOSEPH³ EGGLESTON of Powhatan [a residence], James
City Co., departed this life the 24th day of November, Anno
Domini 1730, aged 52 (or 32) years.

"ANNE EGGLESTON, partner of the above Joseph, of the
aforesaid county, departed this life October 24th, Anno
Domini 1736, aged 34 years.

"The above JOSEPH and ANNE EGGLESTON left behind them
five sons and one daughter, to-wit: Joseph⁴, John⁴, Richard⁴,
William⁴ and Edmund⁴, and Elizabeth⁴, who intermarried with
one William Wyatt, of Caroline Co.

"JOSEPH⁴ EGGLESTON was married to JUDITH, his wife, the
15th of December, 1753, N. S. [new style?], at Urbana, Middlesex Co., by Revd. Barth. Yates. Joseph⁵, son of JOSEPH⁴
EGGLESTON, AND JUDITH, his wife, was born the 24th November, 1754, and was baptized by the Rev. Barth. Yates, the 1st
day of December following.

"Jane[5] Segar, first daughter of JOSEPH[4] EGGLESTON AND JUDITH, his wife, was born the 8th of June, 1756, and was baptized by Rev. John Fox of Gloster county. Anne[5], second daughter of JOSEPH[4] EGGLESTON AND JUDITH, his wife, was born the 24th of February, 1758, and was baptized by the Rev. John Fox, the 18th day of March following. Mary[5], third daughter of JOSEPH[4] EGGLESTON, AND JUDITH, his wife, was born on the 7th of May, 1759, and was baptized by the Rev. John Brumskill the 19th of the same month. Judith[5], fourth daughter of JOSEPH[4] EGGLESTON, AND JUDITH, his wife, was born on the 9th December, 1761, and was baptized by the Rev. John Brumskill the 13th of the same month. Elizabeth[5], fifth daughter of JOSEPH[4] EGGLESTON, AND JUDITH, his wife, was born on 19th April, 1764, and was baptized on the 27th May following by the Rev. John Brumskill, of Raleigh Parish. My dear child Judith departed this life the 29th of April, 1772, of a malignant fever which lasted 14 days.

"JOSEPH[4] EGGLESTON was married a second time to Judith Cobbs (alias) Bently Oct. 18th, 1776, [doubtless Bently was her maiden name], he aged 55 years and she 40 years old. Archibald McRoberts performed the ceremony."

These statements were evidently written by JOSEPH[4] EGGLESTON, and were copied from the books by Mr. Hodijah Meade.

Please notice that Goode states that "Joseph Eggleston of Powhatan or Amelia Co. was perhaps grandson of the first and son of the second" (the Richards), and observe that he moved from "Powhatan" (his residence in) James City Co. to Amelia Co., which accounts for his association with the name Powhatan, and also that, as we have shown, it was the second Joseph[4], who moved to Amelia.

Now we take up again our newspaper article: "He [JOSEPH[3] EGGLESTON] was twice married, his first wife (name unknown) leaving one son, Benjamin Eggleston, who inherited the family mansion of "Powhatan" (James City Co.). His second wife was ANN PETTIS, of Hanover Co., who left five sons: JOSEPH[4], John[4], Richard[4], William[4], and Edward[4], and two daughters, Elizabeth (Betsy) and ———. John[4] and Edward[4] settled in Hanover; Richard[4] in Powhatan; and JOSEPH[4] and William[4] in Amelia Co.

"JOSEPH[4] EGGLESTON, of Amelia, married Judith Segar, of Urbana. John[4], of Hanover, married Betsy Cary. Richard[4] Eggleston married Rebecca Chuff, of Hanover. William[4], of Amelia, married Judith Cary, of Yorktown. Edward[4], of Hanover, married Betsy Wales, of the same county.

"William[4] Eggleston, of Amelia, was father of the following children: William[5] (who never married), Edward[5], Mathew[5], Richard[5], Judith[5] (who married Major Joseph E.), Ann[5] (who married Mr. Hickman), and Joseph[5].

"John[4] Eggleston, of Hanover, left one daughter, who married Mathew Eggleston, from whom are descended the Baptises (sic) and others.

"Richard[4] Eggleston married Miss Chuff, who was the grandmother of Trent Eggleston.

"JOSEPH[4] EGGLESTON, of Amelia, was father of Major Joseph[5] Eggleston, of Egglestetton, Mrs. Jane[5] Cocke, Mrs. Anne[5] Hardaway, MRS. MARY[5] MEADE, and Mrs. Elizabeth[5] Archer.

"Major Joseph[5] Eggleston was first married to Sally Meade, daughter of GENL. EVERARD MEADE. She died at the age of twenty-five leaving three sons, Charles[6], William[6], and Edward[6]. His second wife was Judith Cary Eggleston, his first cousin. She survived him many years, and attained the age of ninety-six. Her children were Francis[6], Edward[6], and Sally[6] Meade.

"The above family record is taken from a paper in possession of Mrs. W. B. Helm and Miss Marianna P. Eggleston, of Carrollton, Carroll Co., Miss."

These items constitute our chief information, and the only uncertainty seems to be about the earliest generations. Notwithstanding the statements to the contrary, it seems certain that Richard Eggleston was the emigrant and first ancestor, and we have adopted this theory in our table. From JOSEPH[3] down there can be no doubt, because we have the definite record of JOSEPH[4]. Benjamin, said to be the son of JOSEPH[3] by his first marriage, could not have been the Benjamin, to whom the land grants of 1690-98 were made, as Joseph[3] was said to have been born in 1678. There is also doubt as to the relationship of the two Richards in our table. But these seem to be our only difficulties, and the later lineage is plain and certain.

And now proceeding with our history, JOSEPH[3] EGGLESTON, our ancestor, married ANNE PETTUS, daughter of DABNEY AND ANNE (OVERTON) PETTUS, of Hanover Co., which links us to the Pettus and Overton families, sketches of whom will follow. The children of this marriage have already been mentioned in the record of JOSEPH[4], our ancestor, he having four brothers and one sister, whose names are recorded in our table.

Of these JOSEPH[4] EGGLESTON, Mrs. Baskervill's ancestor, married on Dec. 11th, 1753, before he removed from "Powhatan", James City Co., to Amelia Co., JUDITH SEGAR, born April 20, 1729, daughter of OLIVER SEGAR, of Middlesex Co., (1684-1741), thus allying us with the Segar family, of whom a sketch will follow. They had at least five children, Joseph[5], Jane[5] Segar, ANNE[5], MARY[5], and Elizabeth[5].

Joseph[5] Eggleston was conspicuous. He was a major in the Revolutionary War. In Howe's *Historical Collections of Virginia* we find: "Major Joseph[5] Eggleston was a native of Amelia Co. He was a highly meritorious officer of Lee's Legion (cavalry), and served through the whole of the southern campaigns. At the conclusion of the war he turned his attention to literature. He was a member of Congress in 1798-9, where he served with credit. He was cut off in the flower of his age by the effects of the amputation of a disordered limb." From Saffel's *Records of the Revolutionary War*, page 288, we learn that "he was second in command in Lee's Legion, Lt. Coln. Henry Lee, 'Light Horse Harry', [father of Genl. Robert E. Lee] being in command."

Major Joseph[5] Eggleston was born in December, 1754, and on March 8th, 1788, married Sally Meade, daughter of GENL. EVERARD[3] MEADE, Mrs. Baskervill's great grandfather, a distinguished soldier of the Revolutionary War, who built The Hermitage in Amelia Co., where he lived, died, and was

buried. Major Eggleston was also the brother of Mrs. Baskervill's great grandmother, MRS. DANIEL HARDAWAY, nee ANNE
EGGLESTON, and MRS. EVERARD[3] MEADE, nee MARY EGGLESTON,
as will appear in our table, she being Genl. Meade's second
wife.

Jane[5] Segar Eggleston on March 5, 1772, married Stephen
Cocke.

ANNE[5] EGGLESTON, born Febry. 4th, 1758, married DANIEL[3]
HARDAWAY, and these two were ancestors of Mrs. Baskervill.

MARY[5] EGGLESTON, born 1759, married 1st on Jany. 23rd,
1779, Benjamin Ward, of Chesterfield Co., and their first child,
Seth[6] Ward, was born Jany. 7th, 1780. Later there was born
to them their daughter, the beautiful Maria[6] Ward, who was
the one love of John Randolph of Roanoke. She declined to
marry John Randolph and afterwards married his kinsman,
Peyton Randolph, who for a short time was acting governor
of Virginia in 1811, after the lamentable death of Governor
Geo. W. Smith in the Richmond theatre fire on Dec. 26th of
that year. But his term lasted only until James Barbour was
elected governor on Jany 31, 1812. He was a son of the
very distinguished Edmund Randolph, governor of Virginia
from 1788 to 1791. Peyton and Maria Ward Randolph were
the parents of Charlotte Randolph, first wife of Dr. John G.
Skelton, Mrs. Baskervill's father, and grandparents of her
sister Mrs. John L. Williams of Richmond, formerly Maria
Ward[8] Skelton. We present a picture of Maria Ward.

Benjamin Ward after a long sickness of eighteen months
died on April 30th, 1783. And later his widow, MRS. MARY
EGGLESTON WARD, married GENERAL EVERARD[3] MEADE (his
second wife), and their son was BENJAMIN[6] L. MEADE, who
married JANE ELIZABETH HARDAWAY. *Their* daughter was
MARIANNE[7] O. MEADE, second wife of Dr. John G. Skelton,
and mother of MRS. BASKERVILL.

Elizabeth[5] Eggleston on May 24th, 1788, married John
Archer, whose father, Coln. Wm. Archer, commandant of the
militia of the county, was conspicuous in the Revolutionary
War. One of his brothers was Lieutenant Joseph Archer,
killed at the battle of Brandywine. John Archer was major in

MARIA WARD

this war, and aide to one of the generals. He was sent to Charlottesville to remove stores in anticipation of a raid from Cornwallis, and was overtaken by the enemy and captured. In the fight he received a sword thrust entirely through his body, but recovered and lived many years. (See Howe's *Virginia*, p. 173).

John and Elizabeth (Eggleston) Archer had four children, viz: William S., Elizabeth, Anne, and Martha, none of whom ever married. Wm. S. Archer was U. S. Senator from Virginia, and was conspicuous. He built in Amelia Co. his beautiful home, "The Lodge", which was very expensive and palatial. Elizabeth died before the Confederate War, and before her brother William. Misses Martha and Anne Archer for many years lived at The Lodge, and were called "The Lodge ladies". They lived to very old age, and died in Richmond, the last of John Archer's family.

And now for the sake of clearness we recapitulate.

The first two generations of our Eggleston table are conjectural, and follow the suggestion of Goode. The two emigrants named Richard, one twenty-four and the other sixteen years old, in 1635, on the ship *"Transport"*, could have been neither father and son, nor brothers; and Richard in the Indian fight of 1656, may or may not have been one of them. Our newspaper article states, that the emigrant, whose name was said to be Joseph, was the father of Joseph Eggleston, who lived at "Powhatan", above Williamsburg, and the second of these may have been either JOSEPH[3] or JOSEPH[4] of our table. Mrs. Judith Eggleston Old's letter states that the emigrant was JOSEPH[3], who married ANNE PETTUS. And these are doubtless the family traditions, which are very often partly correct, partly incorrect. In the absence of definite knowledge we have followed in our table Goode's suggestions merely in a tentative way, with a frank statement of the facts. Placing Benjamin, who patented lands in 1690 and 98 is a mere guess. Goode says that William Eggleston who married Judith Cary, was a son of Joseph[4], who married Judith Segar, but the dates of his birth and marriage show this to be an error, and we have placed him in the previous generation. The remainder of the table seems to be authentic.

In Goode's *Virginia Cousins* we find: "In later generations, writes a friend, the Eggleston family has been noted for the number of magistrates and judges of ability produced by it. The Egglestons have borne a very high reputation for integrity, and a certain clear, unpoetic intelligence. They were serious, stern, usually careful of their money, and hated ostentation and affectation with a sort of passion."

We have no knowledge of the Eggleston family before the emigration to Virginia.

THE SEGAR FAMLY

SEGAR FAMILY TABLE.

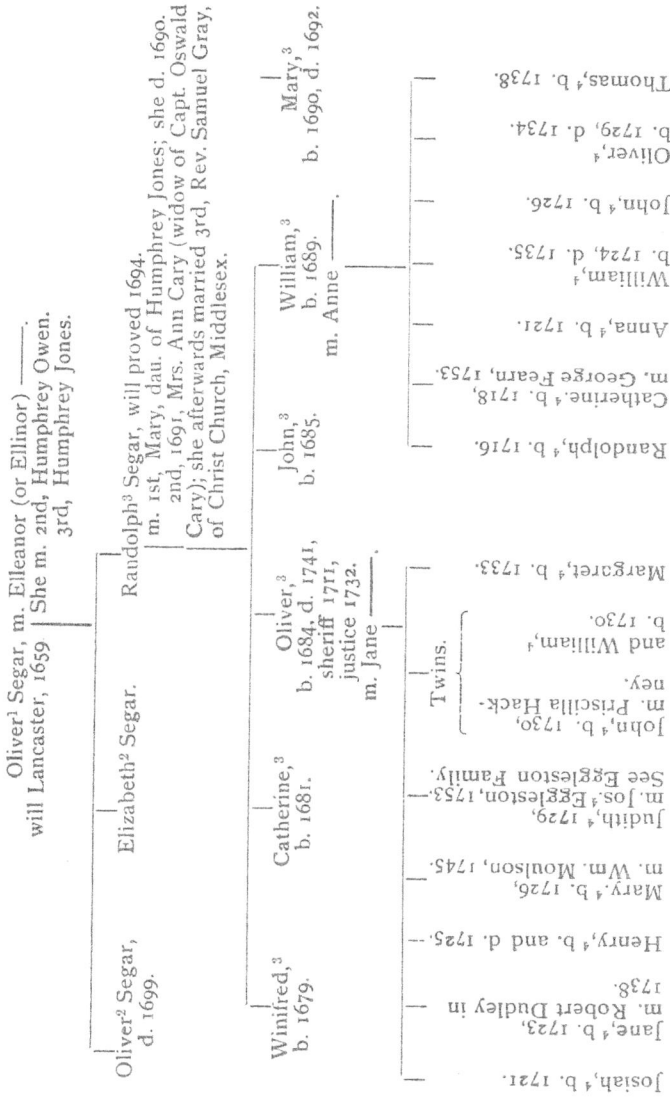

Oliver[1] Segar, m. Elleanor (or Ellinor) —— | She m. 2nd, Humphrey Owen.
will Lancaster, 1659 | 3rd, Humphrey Jones.

Oliver[2] Segar, d. 1699.

Elizabeth[2] Segar.

Raudolph[3] Segar, will proved 1694.
m. 1st, Mary, dau. of Humphrey Jones; she d. 1690.
2nd, 1691, Mrs. Ann Cary (widow of Capt. Oswald Cary); she afterwards married 3rd, Rev. Samuel Gray, of Christ Church, Middlesex.

Winifred,[3] b. 1679.

Catherine,[3] b. 1681.

Oliver,[3] b. 1684, d. 1741, sheriff 1711, justice 1732. m. Jane

John,[3] b. 1685.

William,[3] b. 1689. m. Anne.

Mary,[3] b. 1690, d. 1692.

Children of Oliver[3] (m. Jane):

Josiah,[4] b. 1721.

Jane,[4] b. 1723, m. Robert Dudley in 1738.

Henry,[4] b. and d. 1725.

Mary,[4] b. 1726, m. Wm. Moulson, 1745.

Judith,[4] b. 1729, m. Jos.[4] Eggleston, 1753 — See Eggleston Family.

John,[4] b. 1730, m. Priscilla Hackney. } Twins.

and William,[4] b. 1730.

Margaret,[4] b. 1733.

Children of William[3] (m. Anne):

Randolph,[4] b. 1716.

Catherine,[4] b. 1718, m. George Fearn, 1753.

Anna,[4] b. 1721.

William,[4] b. 1724, d. 1735.

John,[4] b. 1726.

Oliver,[4] b. 1729, d. 1734.

Thomas,[4] b. 1738.

CHAPTER XI

THE SEGAR FAMILY

Judith Segar, born April 20th, 1729, married Joseph[4] Eggleston on December 11th, 1753.

In Lower's *Family Dictionary* we find the following: "Segar, Seagar, ancient Saxon Sigora, a conqueror, Sigor, victorious. An ancient personal name written in *Domesday Book* Segar, Sigar, and Sigarus. In Poitou (France) an eminent local surname, De Sigur." We also find it spelled Seager, and Segur.

In England we find a family of Segars in Devonshire of considerable antiquity, and sufficiently prominent to find a place in the county pedigrees. See Tuckett's *Devonshire Pedigrees*, p. 173. In the *Dictionary of National Biography* in the Virginia State Library we find a record of a member of this family, Francis Segar, or Seager, (flourished 1549-1563), a translator and a poet, who seems to have been quite conspicuous. He published quite a number of books.

Again we find Sir William Segar, d. 1633, who became the garter king-at-arms of England, which seems to have been a high office. The duties include the regulation of the arms of the peers, and he has apartments within Windsor Castle, and very fine decorations, including a crown of gilt, as described in the encyclopedias.

And again we find John Seguare (flourish 1414), a rhetorician and poet, son of a knight of Norwich. These are sufficient to show the good standing and intelligence of the family in England.

We can not trace the Virginia family back to England.

There is a New England family of this name, who have a book of family genealogy, but we have never seen it and know nothing about them.

In regard to the Virginia Segar family we know very little except names and dates.

In the *Virginia Magazine* of the Historical Society, Vol. V, p. 167, we find a short history of the family. The *Parish Register of Christ Church*, Middlesex, copies of which may be found in the Virginia Historical Society library, and in our own library, furnishes a record of the births, baptisms, marriages, and burials of the family. And OLIVER SEGAR's will, dated Jany. 24th, 1658, and probated and recorded in Lancaster Co. on March 30th, 1659, of which we have a copy, furnishes a good deal of information. These three very reliable authorities constitute our chief sources of information. Outside of the will we have little or no knowledge of OLIVER[1] SEGAR.

Lancaster Co. was formed in 1652, and Middlesex was formed from Lancaster in 1675. The clerk of Lancaster writes us that this will is among the oldest records in that office, and that there is nothing to show from what country OLIVER[1] SEGAR came. He names his oldest son Oliver[2], son RANDOLPH[2], wife ELLINOR (sic), and daughter Elizabeth[2]; also friends Nicholas Cocke, and Richard Lee, executors. He showed his English origin by leaving all his houses and lands to his eldest son, Oliver[2] Segar, and all his personal estate was to be equally divided between his wife and three children. All was to remain in the hands of his wife until the children "come to age".

There is a deed of October 30th, 1663, from ELLINOR OWEN to her children, Oliver[2] and RANDOLPH[2] Segar, and Ellinor Owen. Mrs. Segar married secondly Humphrey Owen, who was dead in 1663. She married a third time Humphrey Jones.

The inventory of the son Oliver[2], on record in Middlesex, was dated Nov. 13th, 1699. He was apparently without issue. The names Oliver and Eleanor are spelled in the will Olliver and Ellinor.

RANDOLPH[2] SEGAR, who is mentioned in 1661 as son of OLIVER[1] SEGAR, deceased, married in or before 1693 the administratrix (doubtless the widow) of Capt. Oswald Cary. She married thirdly Rev. Samuel Gray, minister of Christ

Church, Middlesex. Randolph[2] Segar appears to have married first Mary, daughter of Humphrey Jones (of course daughter of another wife than Ellinor), who in his will dated, 1684, named his grandchildren Winifred, Catharine, and Oliver Segar, and his daughter Marie Segar.

The will of RANDLE[2] SEGAR was dated Dec., 1693, and proved in Middlesex in January, 1740; legatee Jane Segar Winifred, and Catherine Segar, sons John[3] and William[3] Segar, and "my father Jones". He owned in Middlesex a plantation called "Jamaica", and others.

In Febry. 1685-6 MRS. MARY SEGAR was the executrix of Humphrey Jones, her father.

The inventory of "MR. RANDOLPH[2] SEGAR" was recorded in Middlesex Febry. 3, 1700.

OLIVER[3] SEGAR (son of RANDOLPH[2]) gave bond as sheriff of Middlesex in June, 1711.

He also was a justice of Middlesex in 1732.

The will of John[3] Segar was dated October, 1729, and proved in Middlesex in January, 1740; legatees Jane Segar Nicholas whole estate; his brothers Oliver and William Segar, and Josiah, son of Oliver Segar, executors.

The inventory of CAPT. OLIVER[3] SEGAR was recorded in Middlesex in July, 1741.

The following marriage bonds are on file in Middlesex:

Catherine Segar and George Fearn, Sept. 4th, 1753; Randolph Segar, security.

Joseph Eggleston and Judith Segar, Dec. 11, 1753.

William Moulson and Mary, daughter of Oliver Segar, July 26th, 1745.

John Segar and Priscilla Hockney, Dec. 17th, 1764.

From these records and from numerous items in the *Parish Register of Christ Church*, Middlesex, too many to record here, we have made our Segar table, which precedes this sketch.

A copy of the items from the *Parish Register* will be found in our *Meade Papers*, Vol. II.

Later we have purchased a copy of this book, which will be found in our library.

THE PETTUS FAMILY

THE PETTUS FAMILY.

Sir John Pettus, Knight, M. P. 1601–1611,
of Norwich England, of The Va. Co.,
d. 1613—SAID TO BE FATHER OF

Coln. Thomas[1] Pettus, m. Mrs. Eliz. Durand.
of Littleton, Va.

Thomas[2] Pettus, Jr., m. 1st, —— Dabney.

John[3] (or Dabney, or John Dabney) Pettus, m. Anne Overton.

Anne[4] Pettus, before 1720, m. Joseph[3] Eggleston.
See Eggleston Table.

CHAPTER XII

THE PETTUS FAMILY

ANNE PETTUS, daughter of JOHN (OR DABNEY) PETTUS, married JOSEPH[3] EGGLESTON.

This seems to be a new line in tracing the Meade connections. We know very little about it, and the first part is uncertain.

"SIR JOHN PETTUS, knight, of England, was one of the signers of the third charter to the Virginia Company in 1612. We are told that he was of Norwich, England, and was a member of parliament from that city in 1601 and 1604-1611, and was a 'benefactor of the Norwich Cathedral'. He died April 9th, 1613." (Brown's *Genesis of America*, pp. 545 and 966). He is said to have been the father of the next, COLN. THOMAS PETTUS, but there is no evidence of the accuracy of this statement.

COLN. THOMAS[1] PETTUS (SR.), of "Little Town", or "Littleton", James City Co., Va., was one of the most conspicuous men of this colony. He was a member of the Governor's Council for many years, certainly between 1642 and 1648 (*Va. Hist. Magazine*, V, 111). In Tyler's *Cradle of the Republic* we are told: "Littletown adjoined Kingsmill on the east, and was on the north side of James River, Kingsmill being just east of Archer's Hope Creek, and not far from Jamestown. In March, 1633, Littletown was the residence of Captain George Menifie, of the Council, one of the greatest merchants in Virginia. He had a garden of two acres on the river side, and it was full of roses of Provence, apple, pear, and cherry trees, the various fruits of Holland, with different kind of sweet smelling herbs, such as rosemary, sage, marjoram, and thyme. He had growing around the house plenty of peach

trees, which astonished his visitors very much; for they were
not to be seen on the coast anywhere else. Here the governor sometimes held court.

"In 1661 Littletown was the residence of COL. THOMAS
PETTUS, *of the Council.* He married ELIZABETH, the widow of
Richard Durant, and after his death she married Capt. John
Grove, who died in 1671. [The place passed to CAPT.
THOMAS PETTUS, JR.]

"Capt. THOMAS PETTUS, JR.'s widow, Mourning [Glen],
married James Bray, Jr., and thus the place passed to the
Bray family till 1752, when on the death of Thomas Bray
Littletown descended to his daughter Elizabeth, who married
Col. Philip Johnson."

In the personal history of this period we are much struck
with two things, that a large proportion of the educated men
were either captains or colonels, and that they needed much
to observe Mr. Weller's advice to "Bevare of vidders."

In an article in the *Times-Ditpatch* of March 5, 1916, con-
firming the account above, it is stated that: "COLN. THOMAS
PETTUS, of York Co., later of Williamsburg, where he was a
vestryman of Bruton Church, married in 1645, ELIZABETH,
widow of Richard Durant, and they had a son, THOMAS PET-
TUS, JR. He married first MISS DABNEY, the mother of his
children, and secondly Mourning Glen, who married secondly
James Bray, of James City Co."

In another article in the same newspaper of Sept. 5th, 1915,
we are told: "ANNE OVERTON married JOHN PETTUS, grandson of COL. THOMAS PETTUS, Councillor of State for Virginia
in 1641-1660."

In a still earlier article in the *Times-Dispatch* of March
15th, 1909, signed "Anna Pettus Eastham", in answer to our
inquiry, it was stated: "ANN PETTUS was the daughter of
DABNEY PETTUS and ANN OVERTON. She was born in Hanover county about 1720-5. She married Eggleston. Issue:
Edward and ANN. She married second time Clivius Duke,
Sr. Issue: Clivius Duke, Jr., and three daughters, Jane, Elizabeth, and Amy. Clivius Duke, Jr., was ancestor of the Dukes
of Albemarle.

"The old Eggleston mansion is still standing on Little River, in Louisa Co."

Later we made an inquiry through the newspaper, stating that the date given for the birth of ANNE PETTUS was too late, as her son JOSEPH EGGLESTON married JUDITH SEGAR in 1753, and his mother must have been born before 1720, and asking for more history of the Pettus family.   But there was no reply.

And now again in another newspaper article of July 10th, 1910, in regard to the Overton family, from which he was descended, Mr. Wilson Miles Cary, a prominent genealogist, states: "ANN OVERTON married JOHN PETTUS, grandson of COL. THOMAS PETTUS, of Littleton, who was Councillor of State for Virginia in 1641-1660."

The question arises; was Mr. Pettus, who married ANN OVERTON, named Dabney or John? The preponderance of evidence seems in favor of John, or his name may have been John Dabney Pettus. Mr. Cary's reputation, as a genealogist, particularly in regard to his own family, carries much weight with it.

From Henning's Statutes, we find that CAPT. THOMAS PETTUS, JR., was also a member of the Council from 1646 to 1660.

Also we find that another Thomas Pettus was Burgess from Lunenburg Co. for 1769-1775, but he was not an ancestor.

Another article in the *Times-Dispatch* of March 5th, 1916, refers to "a very carefully compiled genealogy of the Pettus family sent [to the writer] by a Virginia man," but we have not seen it.

THE OVERTON FAMILY

OVERTON TABLE.

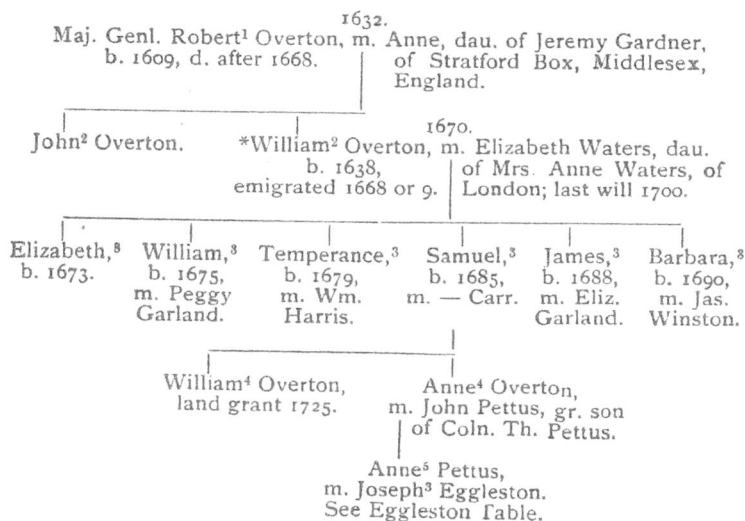

1632.

Maj. Genl. Robert[1] Overton, m. Anne, dau. of Jeremy Gardner,
    b. 1609, d. after 1668. | of Stratford Box, Middlesex,
                               England.

1670.

John[2] Overton.   *William[2] Overton, m. Elizabeth Waters, dau.
                    b. 1638, | of Mrs. Anne Waters, of
           emigrated 1668 or 9. | London; last will 1700.

Elizabeth,[3]	William,[3]	Temperance,[3]	Samuel,[3]	James,[3]	Barbara,[3]
b. 1673.	b. 1675, m. Peggy Garland.	b. 1679, m. Wm. Harris.	b. 1685, m. — Carr.	b. 1688, m. Eliz. Garland.	b. 1690, m. Jas. Winston.

William[4] Overton,   Anne[4] Overton,
  land grant 1725.   m. John Pettus, gr. son
                  | of Coln. Th. Pettus.

Anne[5] Pettus,
m. Joseph[3] Eggleston.
See Eggleston Table.

*The descent of William[2] Overton from General Robert Overton is
said to be doutful, rather conjectural than otherwise.

CHAPTER XIII

THE OVERTON FAMILY

ANNE PETTUS, who married JOSEPH³ EGGLESTON, is said to have been a daughter of DABNEY, or JOHN PETTUS, and his wife, ANNE OVERTON.

There appeared in the genealogical columns of the *Times-Dispatch* of September 5th and 12th, 1915, a very interesting article by Mr. Wilson Miles Cary, a prominent genealogist of Baltimore, dated July 20th, 1910, he having died since that time, in regard to the Overton family, from which he was descended. This article will be found in our *Meade Papers,* Vol. II. It is very comprehensive and full.

Mr. Cary in his article, giving "the family of Samuel² Overton, who married Miss Carr", states: "In the Virginia Land office there is record of a deed for land on 'south and north forks of Elk Creek, 7 January, 1725, to William Overton, son of Samuel Overton, sometime of New Kent county'. It was SAMUEL² OVERTON's daughter ANN³ OVERTON, who married JOHN PETTUS, grandson of COLN. THOMAS PETTUS, of 'Littleton', who was Councilor of State for Virginia, 1641-1660."

We see that this, contradicting our other account, states that JOHN, not Dabney, PETTUS married ANNE OVERTON, and that he was a grandson of COLN. THOMAS PETTUS, of "Littleton", the Councilor of 1641-1660. Mr. Cary, being a descendant and a very skillful genealogist, was probably right. And this settles two points; first that ANNE OVERTON's husband was a grandson of COLN. THOMAS PETTUS, SR., and second that most probably his name was JOHN, and not Dabney, or possibly he may have had both names, thus JOHN DABNEY PETTUS.

We have constructed our Overton table from Mr. Cary's article, clearly stating the rather uncertain descent from MAJOR GENERAL ROBERT OVERTON, of the Cromwell army. This is not authoritative, and seems to be only conjectural, and several points in Mr. Cary's narrative are said to be not sustained. But we give a summary of it, as it is only the first part that seems to be doubtful.

The descent claimed from GENERAL ROBERT OVERTON was lost or unknown in the family until Mr. Cary, having become a professor in the West Virginia University, at Morgantown, met Mr. Robert Carter Berkeley, a retired professor, born in Hanover Co., and descended from the Overtons. From him he learned that the Overtons descended from that officer, of whom Sir Walter Scott wrote in his *"Woodstock"* and *"Old Mortality"*.

Major General Robert Overton was one of the chief officers of Oliver Cromwell's army. The *"Dictionary of National Biography"*, in the Virginia State Library, states that he was born about 1609, married in 1632, and after a distinguished career was imprisoned on the Isle of Jersey until 1668, when all trace of him was lost. He is said to have been of the same family as the famous Bishop William Overton, of Coventry and Litchfield, who was born in London, between 1520 and 1530. "So it is more probable that Robert named one of his sons William." It is suggested that he was exiled to Barbadoes, as Hatton's list of the "Inhabitants of the Parish of Christ Church, Barbadoes, 22 December, 1679," includes "one Robert Overton, living alone, without family and without servants, either black or white, possessing but five acres of land." From this work we also find he was "Son of John Overton, of Easington in Holderness, Yorkshire, born about 1609, admitted to Gray's Inn on 1st November, 1631." He entered the Parliamentary army at the beginning of the Civil War, and became very distinguished, as will be seen from the Cary article. In 1653 he succeeded to the family estate at Easington, returned to England, and became Governor of Hull.

Being very extreme in his views, he was imprisoned and never released, as far as is known.

In 1632 he married ANNE, daughter of JEREMY GARDNER, of Stratford Box, Middlesex, England. His eldest son John was admitted to Gray's Inn on 11th November, 1661. Other interesting details in regard to him may be found in the Cary article.

WILLIAM OVERTON, the first of the name in Virginia, is said to have been a son of this GENL. ROBERT OVERTON, and to have been born in England on December 3, 1638, and to have come to Virginia before 1670. He married ELIZABETH WATERS on November 24th, 1670, at Yorktown, Va., on board the vessel on which she came to this country. She. was the daughter of MRS. ANNE WATERS, of St. Sepulcher's Parish, London, an abstract of whose will may be found in the *Virginia Magazine,* Vol. 11, p. —, she being a widow. Dated September 29th, 1697, and probated in London, England, on July 4th, 1700, it names "son John Waters, who for divers years hath been gone to Virginia, five shillings and no more; son Samuel Waters and Margaret his wife ten shillings apiece; daughter ELIZABETH OVERTON, now in Virginia, ten shillings; and William, her husband, ten shillings; son in law, Mr. William Goodwin, ten shillings for a ring; brother in law, Caleb Millett, ten shillings; son Thomas Waters residuary legatee, and he the sole executor."

It is stated that there was at the recent Jamestown Exposition a small quaintly drawn picture, in the Virginia exhibit, of the landing of "MARY" (ELIZABETH) WATERS with the faithful WILLIAM in the garb of a covenanter ready to receive her. And it is also said that the records of Mathews Co., Va., show that WILLIAM OVERTON paid fifty pounds of tobacco for the passage to Virginia of his fiancée.

The Virginia land books record a deed (or grant) for forty-six hundred acres of land on the south side of Pamunkey River, on Falling Creek, April 23rd, 1681, to William Overton for transporting ninety-two persons to the colony, including ELIZABETH WATERS. Another deed to WILLIAM OVERTON in 1690 was for additional land in St. Peter's Parish.

WILLIAM[2] AND ELIZABETH (WATERS) OVERTON had issue:
Elizabeth[3], b. 28th June, 1673, no trace;
William[3], b. 6th August, 1675, m. Peggy Garland;
Temperance[3], b. 2nd March, 1679, m. Wm. Harris;
SAMUEL[3], b. 14th August, 1685, m. ——— Carr;
James[3], b. 14th August, 1688, m. Elizabeth Garland;
Barbara[3], b. 5th February, 1690, m. James Winston.

Of these our particular interest lies in Samuel[3] Overton, and for the others we refer to the Cary article. Mr. Cary, as previously stated, says: "It was Samuel[3] Overton's daughter, Anne[4] Overton, who married John Pettus, grandson of Coln. Thomas Pettus, of Littleton."

Thus we have arrived at our point of connection with the Overton family, and with ANNE[4] OVERTON our interest is transferred to the Pettus family, already mentioned.

Some days after the appearance of Mr. Wilson Miles Cary's article in regard to the Overtons there appeared a reply signed "Subscriber", in which the descent of William Overton from Cromwell's Genl. Overton is mentioned as "conjectural", and stating that Prof. Thomas R. Price had written an Overton Genealogy, which is doubtless reliable and interesting.

INDEX

INDEX

MEADE NAMES

OTHER NAMES

PLACES, &c.

www.ingramcontent.com/pod-product-compliance
Lightning Source LLC
Chambersburg PA
CBHW070906270326
41927CB00011B/2480